FROM UNDER
A BLAZING ASPEN

Seeking Faith In the Back of Beyond

David Webber

Published in Celebration Of 10 Years Of Presbyterian Mission in the Cariboo

Copyright 2000 © David Webber

ISBN 0-9685797-0-1

Canadian Cataloguing In Publication Data

Webber, David, 1950-
From under a blazing aspen

"Published in celebration of 10 years of Presbyterian mission in the Cariboo" --
t.p. Includes bibliographical references.
1. Webber, David, 1950- 2. Cariboo Presbyterian Church. I. Title.
BX9002.B7W42 1999   285'.271175   c99-910954-5

Unless stated otherwise. all Scripture quotations are from the New Revised Standard Version Bible
(NRSV). Other versions quoted include: the Revised Standard Version (RSV) and the King James Version
(KJV) Bibles. Every effort has been made to obtain permissions from other quoted sources.

"Stealing Easter", "Slip Sliding Away", "Driven From the Light", "Grandpa Charlie's Challenge",
"Brother to a Grasshopper", "It Happens In the Strangest Places", "Isaiah's Eagle Can Swim", "Invisible Currents", "Planning For the Future of the Church", "A Moonset Mindset", "Reflections of a Missionary in Canada", "Reflected Light", "Winter Speculation", "Something Old, Something New", and
"Coming Face to Face With a Monster" appeared previously in the *Presbyterian Record.* "Tending to
the Heart Springs" appeared previously in *The 100 Mile Free Press* and the *Presbyterian Record.* "Advice to a Neophyte" and "Maybe You Learn Something Too" appeared previously in *Practice Of Ministry In Canada.* "Treasure The Reminders Of Your Brokenness" appeared previously in The Canadian
Cancer Society's *The Human Spirit.*

Cover Design: Ewa Pluciennik, Avart Design
Editorial Services: Kedre Murray
Printed and bound in Canada by GF Murray Company, Vancouver BC

2nd printing

Printed on acid-free paper. Cover includes 30% post-consumer fibre.

Published by: Webber Ink,
                  RR#1, C17, Dunsmuir Road
                  Lac la Hache, BC V0K 1T0

Earth's crammed with heaven

And every common bush afire with God;

But only he who sees, takes off his shoes,

The rest sit round it and pluck blackberries....

from "Aurora Leigh", Elizabeth Barrett Browning

FOREWORD

I grew up in the back of beyond. I have lived, worked and played there for most of my life. With a little luck I will die there. The back of beyond is my home. In the words of the late John Denver, "Thank God I'm a country boy."

Being a country person has had a pronounced effect upon how I have approached most things in life. It has also had a major effect on how most things in life have approached me. How God and I got tangled together is a perfect example.

The first time I was ever in a church was the day I married Linda. I didn't become a regular church attendee until ten years after that. I was nearly thirty years old before I was fully pew-broke. This is not to say that I grew up without faith, only that the faith I grew up with was unfettered by the church.

I prayed every day since I was as young as I can remember. God was a central part of my life as a child, teen and adult. That I grew up knowing God completely outside the church and in the country begs the question: how was the gift of faith given to me? The answer has two parts.

Grandma taught me about God and prayer from the Bible. Although I didn't read the Bible myself until I was 30, Grandma frequently read it to me as a child. And Grandma taught me about relating to God personally through prayer. But I needed more.

That "more" I received from nature. Nature was everywhere around me. Wild lands, plants and animals were deeply woven into the tapestry of my life. I don't know why, but I was never able to take nature for granted. Neither was I ever satisfied with identifying it and understanding it as a natural historian does. For me, from the earliest age, there was something deeply spiritual about all of nature. There was some deep connection between the God of Grandma's Bible, my own prayers and all of natural creation. God was somehow able to commune with me through nature, in much the same way an artist is able to speak through the medium of his or her art, in much the same way Moses could hear God from the middle of a blazing bush. And so by living with nature, by being immersed in it, God and I carried on together to the point where Christ eventually claimed my life in my 29th year.

God and I are still carrying on together this way. For the past ten years it has been in the Cariboo country, where The Presbyterian Church in Canada sent me and my family as missionaries. Our task was to begin to serve rural people by forming a congregation of house churches scattered across the Cariboo region in central BC. This congregation of rural house churches is called the Cariboo Presbyterian Church, now ten years old. This collection of writing is the product of ten grand years of carrying on with God in the back of beyond in the Cariboo. It is published in celebration of the tenth anniversary of the Cariboo Presbyterian Church. All the profits from the sale of this printing will go to this mission.

David Webber
Lac la Hache, BC
Spring, 1999

Acknowledgements

Many people have encouraged me in my storytelling as the years have passed. They seemed to see some value in what I was doing. I must acknowledge some of those who were most influential. John Congram, the editor of the *Presbyterian Record* and Jim Taylor, late the editor of *Practice Of Ministry In Canada*, have been very kind to me over the years. The people with whom I share the Cariboo Presbyterian Church have also been important in encouraging me to continue telling stories. My partners in mission for the past five years, John Wyminga and Shannon Bell-Wyminga, have affirmed me in many ways and have often done double duty while I was off somewhere writing. Most important of all is my spouse, Linda, who is my staunchest supporter and my harshest critic.

Many of the pieces contained in this small book have appeared, either in total or in part, in other places. I acknowledge these stout-hearted publishers with thanks. The rest of the articles are new and previously untested!

Dave Webber
Spring 1999
Lac la Hache, BC

TABLE OF CONTENTS

SUMMER

Fall

FROM UNDER A BLAZING ASPEN

It happened again this year. It is almost as predictable as the seasons of the year. Winter is a Canadian reality that is preceded by another Canadian season called fall. In my personal calendar, fall is a distinct season from the one which precedes it called autumn, giving the Webber calendar five seasons instead of the four found on the lesser calendars of most people. Fall is absolutely the worst season of the year. Autumn is the best. Autumn is filled with bright days of glorious colours, the invigorating sounds of migrating birds, and the wonderful final harvest of bountiful gardens. And then comes fall clad in its naked trees, blustery winds, drizzling grey rains, dead grass and rotting vegetation. One could say that fall is for the birds, except any bird with an ounce of brains has fled south to escape it. Ahead looms what seem like ten months of winter to be followed by two more of hard sledding. Gawd, it depresses me.

It really does depress me. I don't know if it is the decreasing light conditions or the dead and dying vegetation lying around smelling of decay, or if it is that fall is when I have to pull my fishing boat out of the water. Whatever it is, fall really does coincide with a depression that embraces my soul each year. It happened again this year.

Something else happened again this year. I went for my usual fall forage through the forest back of where we live. I was trying to find some sanity to get me through the horrid depression. I don't know what it is that I look for in this meandering through summer's grave-yard, but I always seem to do it. I set out with my wool cap pulled down over my ears, my warmest wool mackinaw buttoned up tightly, my glasses streaked with grey fog and my teeth set in grim determi-nation. I wander around blinded by the darkness of depression, my only comfort being that others have gone before me. Others like Winston Churchill, who often wrestled with the "black dog", as he called it.

This year my black wanderings led me to a strange encounter with Nature's pulpit. Somewhere in the back of beyond there is a small depression with a marvelous aspen tree growing in it. I noticed the tree even in my mental fog and felt drawn to her as though she was the Tree of Life. The hollow in the landscape must have sheltered her from the frost and the wind for she was still fully clad in her flaming yellow heart-shaped leaves. She was an oasis of colour in a desert landscape. I eased down the slope to sit under her. It was as bright under her fluorescent yellow foliage as a midsummer's day. I sat in silence, enjoying the bright colour and refreshing rustle of her leaves. As I sat, time lost all meaning and a curious feeling began to seep into my being. I caught myself humming a strain of praise. The blackness covering me seemed to lift from my countenance like the early morning mist lifting from a lake embraced by the warmth of the rising sun. It was a grand Presbyterian experience akin to Moses and the burning bush. I was bathed in release. The words of Paul came to me, as if proclaimed from a pulpit draped with a fall of blazing leaves, blazing but not consumed:

> "Finally, beloved, whatever is true, whatever is honorable, whatever is just, whatever is pure, whatever is pleasing, whatever is commendable, if there is any excellence and if there is anything worthy of praise, think about these things. Keep on doing the things that you have learned and received and heard and seen in me, and the God of peace will be with you." (Phil.4:8-9)

Words of a man imprisoned to a people persecuted. Hmmm!

Some of us have difficult lives and live them easily. Others of us have easy lives and live them with difficulty. Depression is often the difference. Yes, there are all kinds of depressions and all kinds of informed theories about their causes. There is also very important medical help that can heal or at least ease the struggle. What came to me from the proclamation under the blazing aspen tree was an awareness of how much a sense of space can influence how I am feeling, both spiritually and emotionally. It is liberating to discover that I have some power over my times of depression. For me at least, this control has to do with deliberately placing myself in places and spaces where colours and light and people and awareness point me to God. It doesn't take much sometimes. Perhaps placing myself under the brightness of an aspen tree will be the catalyst one time. Perhaps placing myself in the brightness of a fellowship of praise will be the catalyst the next. Whatever the case, as I face the coming bleakness of winter, I am going to intentionally look for these places and spaces. And I am going to rest and ruminate there for awhile. Here comes one now. It's Sunday morning.

A MOONSET MINDSET

I was up early, as is my custom. The sun was coming up as the moon was going down. Sunrises always grasp my attention, but not today. Today it was the moonset. I was at the kitchen sink when I noticed it, a great yellow ball about twice its normal size, seemingly balancing itself on the spires of firs and pines on the skyline. A tiny fat cloud sat atop the moon like a Cariboo cowboy's hat pushed back. The lake in the foreground was perfectly calm, reflecting a mirror image of the oversized harvest moon in its waters. It was a scene that put the sunrise happening at exactly the same time and on the opposite skyline to shame. It demanded a photograph.

I padded over to the closet in my bare feet. The floor was cold, so I looked for my buckskin moccasins and pulled them on. Sleepily I rummaged for the camera case, fumbled for the 35mm Canon in its innards, groped for the lens cover and squinted through the sleep still in my eyes to see if there was any film. A few seconds later I was at the patio doors ready to record this amazing moonset.

But it was gone! All that was left was a silver sliver peeking through the crowns of the distant trees. In the few snoozy moments it took me to grab my Canon, the moon had gone ahead without me, leaving me with nothing to shoot. I sat on the couch and mused for a few moments about how fast life slips by, how irreversible time really is and how little control we humans have over just about anything. Later that same morning, someone sang a Leonard Cohen song on the radio and one verse leapt out at me. It went something like: "To those who cringe at what you cannot control, it begins with your family and ends with your soul."

I think it is the reality of how little I can control the stuff of life which causes me more spiritual and emotional discomfort than anything else. Yes, I do have my free will. Yes, I can make choices. And, yes I can, through making choices, have an influence on some aspects of my life. But I also live with other people who make choices that affect my life directly. I can't control their choices. I live in a society that makes choices at hundreds of different levels. I can't control any of that. I live in a world that economically and politically has dramatic effects on me. I can't control any of that either. I live on a planet that has its own set of laws when it comes to turning around the sun and setting the parameters of time, bringing forth weather patterns, causing geological episodes -- all of this having direct influence upon me, all of this beyond my control.

Beyond my control but not beyond God's control. I love the Psalms perhaps better than all the rest of that wonderful Word we call the Bible. Listen to what the Psalmist says.

About personal choices that have gone awry:

"I waited patiently for the Lord, He inclined to me and heard my cry. He drew me up from the desolate pit, out of the miry bog, and set my feet upon a rock, making my steps secure. He put a new song in my mouth..." (Ps.40:1-3a).

About the choices of others that press us down:

"The wicked watch for the righteous, and seek to slay them. The Lord will not abandon them to their power." (Ps.37:32-33a)

About the politics of the world:

"God is our refuge and strength, a very present help in trouble." "Be still and know that I am God. I am exalted among the nations, I am exalted in the earth!" "The Lord of hosts is with us, the God of Jacob is our refuge." (Ps.46:1 & 10-11)

About time and creation:

"Yours (God's) is the day, also the night, You established the luminaries and the sun. You have fixed all the bounds of the earth, You made summer and winter" (Ps.74:16-17).

Over and over in the Psalms what I hear is that ultimately it is God who is in control. The notion of a sovereign God seems to be the Psalmist's main theme. If God is in control...and if God's nature is one of love, grace and faithfulness to those who love Him...what does it matter if I am not in control? In fact, it seems to me the vulnerability that I so often feel around control could best be dealt with by giving up my battle for control and surrendering to God. I think that is the mindset I will take from my recent encounter with the setting moon.

I think I just heard the Psalmist say, "Amen!"

OSPREY EYES

"WATCH OUT!" I screamed the warning as I tried to wedge myself under the thwart of our Chestnut wood-canvas canoe.

"What on earth was that?" Linda asked from the braver vantage point of the canoe seat. We had just pushed off from our dock on the lake and the water was as smooth as silk. Then out of nowhere had come the sound of wind rushing directly over our heads, culminating in a horrendous splash just a few meters from our canoe.

"Well, would you look at that," whispered Linda. I crawled out from my foxhole under the thwart just in time to see one of our local fish hawks, better known to birdwatchers as an osprey, unglue itself from the surface of the water and heavily begin to fly away with a nice-sized fish in its talons. After it turned into the wind and gained several meters in altitude, it stopped flying and shook the water off itself in free fall, looking comically more like a soaked Labrador retriever than any bird. With its aerodynamics restored it quickly gained altitude, clutching its catch close to its body. It circled high to fly directly above our heads, as if to brag about its fishing success.

Suddenly there was a piercing scream. Out of nowhere came a flash of brown and white streaking down on the osprey from out of the sun. The screaming bald eagle hurtled by the osprey, who was turned completely over by the force of the dive. The osprey squawked like a chicken and hastily let go of its breakfast. The eagle popped its wings in parachute fashion, checked its flight, turned over on its side and grabbed the fish in its yellow talons as the fish tumbled towards the sanctuary of the lake. I shook my fist at the arrogant eagle and watched with sympathy as the osprey flew down the lake. It seemed the sympathy was wasted, for the osprey just continued to soar and fish as though nothing had happened.

And so we continued fishing, or at least I tried to. Mostly, I continued thinking about the osprey. The scene I have just described is one Linda and I have witnessed, in one version or other, a hundred times since coming to share the waters of Lac la Hache with the osprey and eagle. After an eagle encounter, the osprey always just continued to soar and fish. There was no plotting against the eagle, no fighting back, no expression of aggression or anger that I could ever perceive. When Osprey's living and fishing was turned upside down by Eagle, Osprey just righted herself and got on with living and soaring and fishing.

Once I thought I had it figured out. I supposed it was the pressure of her hungry clutch at home that denied Osprey the luxury of anger or revenge. But alas, I observed the eagle fiasco several times in the spring, long before there were young in the nest. Osprey always continued to soar and fish. I could never see the point. Obviously the osprey, whose eyesight is reported to be a hundred times better

than mine, can see something in its peaceful response to the screaming eagles in its life that is lifegiving -- some benefit in being a bird
of focus rather than fracas.

She has much gospel to teach me, this osprey. One of the teachings
of Jesus that I have never been able to sink my talons into is the one
about turning the other cheek. It is nicely nested in "The Sermon on
the Mount" in Matthew (Mt.5:39) and "The Sermon on the Plain" in
Luke (Lk.6:29). It is surrounded by other sayings about loving en-
emies and doing good to those who hate you or otherwise rip you off.
I have always felt that this section should be preceded with a beati-
tude of my own composing: 'Blessed are the doormats for they shall
be trod upon.' This section of the Bible concerning a radically pas-
sive response to aggression has usually been treated as either the
basis of some kind of "holy" social ethic for Christian societies or an
impossible commandment for Christian individuals. Whatever the
spin given it by preachers and theologians, I have never been able to
personally appropriate it as gospel. I have never seen any good news
in it that applied to me and the living of my life. Never, that is, until
I began to contemplate the osprey.

Recently I have noted quite a few screaming eagles dive-bombing
me. I am speaking figuratively of situations and individuals that
streak into the living of my life and turn me completely upside down.
Although there is usually a real and critical influence on a particular
day, realistically the disturbance seldom goes beyond the moment.
However, after the moment is over I tend to spend countless hours
and precious mental and spiritual energy brooding about what I could
have done or should have said. I spend more than a modicum of

time replaying the incident, fuming in anger and frustration. Sometimes I even go the second mile of actually plotting and acting to get even. In all of this, my capacity to live life to its fullest is swallowed up for days in stewing, brooding, fuming, plotting and anger. When I compare my response to the screaming eagles in my life with the response of the osprey's to the screaming eagles in hers, I begin to see the picture. I begin to understand the good news in turning the other cheek.

Whatever else Jesus means when he teaches "turn the other cheek", contemplating the osprey has taught me that Jesus has a blessing for me when I do what he says. The blessing is to limit how much these situations or people can disturb and destroy my capacity for living and loving and caring...the stuff of life that brings peace. When I can accept that life is going to have a few screaming eagles and the way to deal with them is to just get on with the rest of life, I will have seen with osprey eyes and gained the capacity to soar in my life.

REFLECTIONS OF A MISSIONARY IN CANADA

I am sitting in the mosquito porch of the one-room log cabin which is my home away from home this week. The smell of fall pervades the crisp bright air of late September. On the edge of the lake, I can hear a chorus of Canada geese and the feeding cackle of several flocks of mallards.

Behind me the crackle of the wood cookstove reminds me of my source of heat. This isolated fishing lodge on Anahim Lake in the Chilcotin area of British Columbia's Cariboo country should be a place of contentment for me this night. But it is not. I'm plagued by a nagging notion that has stuck with me like a hacking cough ever since I took up my appointment as missionary to the Cariboo region of British Columbia.

What is mission in Canada? Normally, I work to begin rural house churches in the Cariboo. This week, however, I am teaching forest ecology and silviculture to a group of native people of the Ulkatcho band, part of the Carrier Nation. The band is attempting to form a forestry crew to better manage their Reserve forest land. In the process, they hope to help some band members out of various cycles of dependency.

I was a teacher of forestry before God reincarnated me as an ordained missionary. My old career allows me to easily assist the Ulkatcho people in their forestry endeavours. But is it mission? What I'm doing here this week has absolutely nothing to do with church programs or church growth or church extension. I will not use my theological training and ordination to the ministry of Word and Sacraments. No one will sing a hymn, knock together a church building or establish a church school. The Presbyterian Church in Canada will not add one extra person to a pew because of my activity.

The native band needed help and I responded. It all seems so ordinary, so non-religious. The band hopes that the project of which I am a small part will help rehabilitate people's lives as well as Reserve land. I hope that somehow my mission superintendent will understand my actions this week.

As I sit here in the infant darkness, furiously smoking my pipe, I find myself wishing I served overseas. Ministries such as mine this week are easily understood as mission "over there." But in Canada, what qualifies as mission? My theological education hasn't equipped me to answer that question. The course list at theological school didn't list missiology. My national church hasn't anything to help me either. We don't have a working mission statement for Canada, to my knowledge -- at least not anymore -- or at least not yet.

A Home Mission Board ceased to exist several decades ago. And instead of a mission statement we have "Operation Guidelines": rules for church institutions in Canada. In addition, if I look at my church's practice in Canada, I see an almost total emphasis on perpetuating the church institution: church growth, successful and attractive church programs, church extension and the like. Is mission in Canada limited to the self-perpetuation of the institutional church?

Jesus commanded:

> "Go therefore and make disciples of all nations, baptizing them in the name of the Father and of the Son and of the Holy Spirit" (Matthew 28:19).

That sounds like "go and grow". If this great commission was all Christ said, then our self-perpetuation mode in Canada would be okay. I suppose.

But Jesus also said:

> "Truly I tell you, just as you did it to one of the least of these who are members of my family, you did it to me" (Matthew 25:40).

Mission in Canada also involves seeking out the brothers and sisters of Jesus and standing with them in ordinary, selfless, Christ-like, healing ways. Standing with sisters and brothers of Jesus with no church institutional agenda.

Tomorrow is another day. The night has matured to ink black. My pipe burns hot and sour from all my frantic puffing and thinking. My bed beckons. Even the gaggle of geese has turned in for the night. Maybe tomorrow I will be able to recognize the six people in the forestry training program on the Reserve as sisters and brothers of Jesus. Maybe tomorrow I will be satisfied with helping them in ordinary, tangible ways. Maybe tomorrow I'll recognize and accept this is mission in Canada.

TREASURE THE REMINDERS OF YOUR BROKENNESS

The Psalmist says something in the 119th Psalm that has a tendency to stick in my throat. Verse 71 of that Psalm reads:

> "It is good for me that I was afflicted, that I might learn thy statutes" (RSV).

I don't like to think of trial and affliction in a positive light, but the Psalmist speaks so a number of times. The Psalm leaves me wondering, do I need to take a closer look at my own personal times of affliction?

Most of us would probably admit that adversity, trial and affliction are what drives us to seek God. In fact, many of us would go so far as to admit that our relationship with God follows the Biblical cycle of apostasy, affliction, repentance, the seeking of God and deliverance. This pattern is most notably recorded in the second chapter of Judges. The problem is that, in Biblical times and today, the pattern seems to repeat itself over and over again.

I don't know about you but I do know a little bit about myself. When things in my life are going smoothly I tend to find myself with less and less time for God. I begin to fall away from Him. Sooner or later brokenness and adversity seem to find me. After a time of trying to deal with it on my own and finding myself inadequate, I turn willingly to God. Of course, I find God always willing and able to walk through brokenness and adversity with me. Gripping God's hand firmly I begin to know God and learn of God's nature. I begin to develop a personal relationship with my Lord. I begin to find new life.

But what happens after I am delivered from the trial? As is so often the tendency, the human reaction to any adversity and affliction is to turn from it and run back towards what is considered to be normalcy. I know I've done that. It is almost as though I run, shaking my head, trying to dislodge even the faintest reminder of my affliction or the resulting brokenness. Before long I am struggling to live my life as before, tending to fall away from God, and I suppose, ready to repeat the cycle.

There was one time when this cycle was interrupted for me. It was twenty years ago and I am still powerfully affected by it. Shortly after my twenty-ninth birthday I was diagnosed as having cancer. The illness, with the resulting chemotherapy and radiotherapy that continued for almost a year and a half, left me broken physically, mentally and spiritually. Words cannot describe the experience. But it was not all bad. It seemed that being wounded acted like a catalyst. I found myself on my face before God in complete and total surrender. Never had I, or have I since, experienced such a closeness with God. He met me in my afflicted state, walked with me and eventually, in answer to prayer and using the healing gifts of modern medicine, he re-established me in health.

As I regained my health, I wanted to run back to normalcy as fast as I could. I wanted to forget that I had ever had the disease. I wanted to get on with living as I had before I became sick. The problem was that I couldn't. Every time I encountered certain smells and tastes, saw the same people or faced similar situations, I would remember the disease and the brokenness. With the memories came fear and depression. I prayed continuously for God to deliver me from my own memory. The prayers seemed to go unanswered. Then one day, while doing a study of the book of Judges, I received an answer to my prayer (Judges Ch. 2). The answer was not what I expected, but then God is never limited by my expectations. Neither the reminders of my brokenness nor the fears were taken away. However, like the apostle who was shown the Godly purpose of the thorn in his flesh, I was given insight into my illness and its painful reminders. I was shown the blessedness of poverty of spirit.

What became clear was that for me and my cousins in the book of Judges, the path to becoming a person of God was in recognizing one's inadequacy to deal with the stuff of life, including death. If the path to this awareness comes through affliction and its accompanying brokenness, then could I not say with the Psalmist: "It was good for me that I was afflicted that I might learn thy statutes" (Ps. 119:71)? It is good that I have suffered that I might walk closer with my Lord. If the wounds of life cause me to seek my God, then do not the reminders of those wounds drive me to cling to Him?

I am persuaded that brokenness can be an instrument God may use to draw me to Himself. I am beginning to learn to treasure the reminders of my brokenness, for the Lord can use them to prevent me from going backwards in my faith journey. More than that, I am beginning to treasure the reminders of my brokenness because God can use them to put me in compassionate solidarity with a wounded friend that I might be a fellow traveller in the journey towards wholeness in God. The saying is trustworthy and true: "With God nothing is impossible."

PLAYFUL LIKE A FOX

I had been sitting for almost three hours waiting for a nice bit of venison to present itself. We needed the winter's meat and I needed the refreshment of doing something primeval. I had found a good deer trail and I was quite sure that if I sat beside it for long enough a nice big buck would offer himself up for our family larder. The problem was that so far it seemed I was the only one on board with my plan. That was when I first noticed the movement.

Perhaps half a kilometer away a red flash crossed the trail. Then there was another flash, this time something black. It was not a deer, but anything to watch was an improvement over what had been available so far. The binoculars became my eyes.

About 200 meters away the red and black flashes appeared again. This time they intersected the trail and proceeded to walk slowly down it towards me. The flashes developed into a couple of foxes, one a red and the other a silver (black with gray guard hairs).

I watched them intently, willingly forgetting about my deer hunting. They walked one behind the other, going from one side of the trail to the other, exploring everything imaginable. Soon they were within 30 meters of my deer blind. The wind was blowing from their backs, depriving their olfactory senses of the slightest idea that I was in the vicinity.

The red fox, a male with a grizzled muzzle, spotted a fresh hill of horse dung on the edge of the trail. He went over and examined it with great interest. After smelling and looking at the large moist pile from every angle, he lay down beside it and stared at it as if considering what kind of animal could have made such a deposit. He stood, stretched, and with a most disgusted expression on his face concerning the deterioration of the neighbourhood, cocked his leg all over the fresh horse evidence.

The silver fox, a younger female, watched the performance from a short distance. When the thinking and critical commentary were done she came dancing over towards the old red male. She dove over him and then under him several times. He chased her at full speed around a circle two meters in diameter. Suddenly they stopped and smelled noses. Just as suddenly she chased him around the same circle but in the opposite direction. Then, for no apparent reason, the female careened off the trail like a winged duck to hide in the bush. The older male gave her a few seconds before tearing off in search. When he found her, an insane chase ensued back and forth across the trail.

And then it was over. With the same intensity as they played, they stopped and collapsed. The female lay down panting in the long grass beside the trail. The male flopped down beside her, resting his head on her back, content with a job well done.

From Under a Blazing Aspen

I chuckled to myself thinking: silly fox mating ritual. But my knowledge of foxes would not allow me to be so easily dismissive. These two foxes were not mating. This was October. Mating season for foxes was not for several months. These two gadabouts were quite simply, but very seriously, playing. In so doing they were obviously realizing and enjoying their created purpose. And I could feel their Creator's pleasure.

Playing. As I watched the dozing duo I reflected: is there another word so far removed from my Christian vocabulary or experience of faith? Words like "struggle", "wounded", "broken" and "pain" are often used when I talk about faith. Plodding words like "pilgrimage", "walk" and "journey" I often use to describe my progress in faith. Dutiful words like "worship", "faithfulness", "study" and "prayer" I always use to describe my relationship with faith. But I don't think I have ever used the word "play" or any of its derivatives in the same sentence as the word or concept of faith. And faith has everything to do with my relationship with my Creator God. What a strange revelation, I thought as I continued to spy on the foxes.

A rumpled old raven came flying down the trail and interrupted my thoughts. He was gliding and swooping about 30 meters above the tops of the tall Douglas fir trees. My binocular-clad eyes were drawn from the foxes up to the gliding raven. Like ravens are wont to do when bored, this one croaked several times like a dying frog. Then, right in my binoculars, Raven did something I had never witnessed before. Raven swooped upward and then turned and flew completely upside down for a couple of seconds. When he had righted himself, he cawed with great glee and swooped upwards and repeated the aerobatics maneuver again, and again. The raven was having a gas playing, right in the middle of my serious theological reflections. A sign from God? Perhaps, I thought.

My mind wandered off into Scripture as I sat silently among God's playing critters. Is there any Biblical evidence for play as a spiritual thing -- an expression of faith? Or is play, as my own Puritan experience would seem to indicate, quite separate from faith? One Biblical story came to mind. It was the story of David dancing before the Lord as all the house of Israel, with great shouting and trumpet music, ushered the ark of the Lord into the city of Jerusalem. The story relates how David was engaged in this act of spiritual playfulness with all his might, leaping and dancing before the Lord. When Michal, David's wife, ridiculed his actions, saying he had exposed himself in his exuberance to the maids of his own servants, David insisted that his playful dancing was an act of faith offered to God, not the maids, and therefore his actions would be held in esteem (2Samuel 6:12ff).

David is noted in Scripture as "a man after God's own heart". As Biblical time progresses, David becomes the paradigm for Messiah, which we Christians believe Jesus of Nazareth fulfills. Even Jesus, when I think about it, shows no distinction between faith and playfulness. In fact, he is criticized by the puritanically religious Pharisees of his day for playing too much and with the wrong kinds of people.

As I watched the sunlight and my friends the foxes fade out of sight, it became clear to me in my reflection that I am more like those religious Pharisees and less like King David and Jesus than I ought to be. Somehow, I must discover the grace in my Christian spirituality to become playful like a fox.

PLANNING FOR THE FUTURE OF THE CHURCH?

It is fall and almost the end of another year. More than that, it is almost the end of a century. For anyone who takes the church seriously these are times when one is compelled to think long and write hard about the future of the church in the twenty-first century. What should it be like? How should it change? How should it stay the same? And so I find myself spending this fall evening sitting befor a crackling fire reflecting on an article that someone has asked me to write, "Planning For the Future Of the Church".

As I struggle with the title I find it perturbs me. Perhaps it is because, in tone, it seems to fit a developing negative pattern for much of the Christian church in Canada. This pattern has been plaguing my own Presbyterian denomination since the disruption of 1925. It has to do, paradoxically, with a survival mentality on one hand and a success ethic on the other. In the past 15 years I have witnessed at least two examples of this disturbing phenomenon in my own church, "The Double In The 80's Campaign" and "The Live The Vision Campaign". Both of these movements were driven by a concern for church survival and success. Unfortunately my denomination is in good company, as it seems to me a similar trend is unfolding across the Church catholic. Somehow we must stop these trends for the sake of faithfulness to Christ. We must seek an entirely new direction. In seeking this new direction, I believe that as a minimum, the following rethinking should take place.

1. We must begin to believe our Bibles. No, I am not arguing for a simple literal interpretation. What I am arguing for is, after we have done all of our faithful Biblical interpretation, we must believe what God is saying to us through his Word. We continually are asking the question, What must the church be doing? We feign listening to Scripture but we act as though all of Scripture is puzzling and difficult to understand. Granted, there are parts of Scripture which are puzzling. However, in the words of Peter Marshall in his sermon, *By Invitation Of Jesus*:

"...our problems are not centered around the things we don't understand, but rather in the things we do understand, the things we could not possibly misunderstand. This, after all, is but an illustration of the fact that our problem is not so much that we don't know what we should do. We know perfectly well... but we don't want to do it." [1]

Beginning to believe and act upon what the Scriptures are saying requires that we begin to proclaim powerfully and listen communally. In my opinion, the church has become plagued with impotent and flatulent preaching aimed at giving individuals a warm fuzzy. We mistakenly call this the pastoral preaching of grace. I believe our theological schools must produce graduates with greater skill in powerful, faithful and prophetic proclamation. Believing takes hearing.

2. I believe we must liberate the Scriptures from individualistic listening and begin to listen to them as a community of faith: to listen not just for what God is saying to me but for what God is saying to us. This, after all, is the context out of which most of Scripture came. To be faithful to that context we need to form faith groupings where the Word is interpreted in community. Small groups are essential to this. Small groups must become the listening centre of our congregations rather than the collectivities that we mistakenly call communities, namely the Sunday morning congregation.

3. I have torn my Bible apart and I can find no place where it says anything about the church having a future that belongs to it. The Bible, it seems to me, is very clear in stating over and over that the future belongs to Christ, not the church. The Bible is also very clear that the church is to lose itself in seeking, following and serving Christ for the world, seeking first the Kingdom. Tullio Vinay, the founder of the Agape movement in the Waldensian church, put it succinctly when he said, "The church's task is not to save itself.... it is rather to give itself in love and service.... in fact to die for the world".[2]

It seems to my simple country mind that the first thing we have to come to terms with in planning for the church's future is realizing that it doesn't have one. The church only has Christ's future (the Kingdom of God) and selflessly serving Christ in Christ's future. Christ's future has to do first with his reign of Shalom for the world. The church as Christ's body exists for the world, not the world for the church. The church is not the Kingdom, it is the servant people of the Kingdom. Anything that a church does in which the prime motive is to selfishly ensure its survival or to bless itself with growth and success in the world, believing that this has to do with ushering in the Kingdom of God, is unfaithful. Upon reflection, perhaps campaigns like "Doubling In The Eighties" and "Live The Vision" qualify, at least at one level, as unfaithfulness to Christ. We must begin to understand that in faithfulness, motive is everything.

4. If we listen to Scripture faithfully and communally concerning the call to selfless service on behalf of Christ for the world, how can we justify that we have become brokers of power and real estate? As a church, we must find other, more faithful, models of ministry that will free us from the temptation to serve ourselves through the procurement of property and institutional survival or success. We need to discover the liberty in not owning buildings. We need to discover the freedom of not having large congregational or denominational bureaucracies. Models of ministry such as the house church and base Christian communities are both ancient and contemporary ways to liberate the body of Christ for service. We must find more such models of ministry for use in Canada. We must begin to embrace and celebrate smallness and simplicity in these models.

5. Much of what we have put our energy into in the past two decades has been aimed at the suburban upper middle class. In fact, my denomination's recent "Live The Vision" campaign made no bones about predicating its fundraising drive on the supposed fact that the Presbyterian Church in Canada is called to serve the Canadian intellectual upper middle class. The bulk of funds raised were to be spent in Canada to serve the suburban middle class. When Christ says to love and serve the poor and oppressed first, he means

exactly that. So what business do we have maintaining with pride that we are a church called to serve the intellectual upper middle class? Are there no poor or oppressed in Canada? We close down churches in the economically pressed inner city and rural communities so we can open churches in middle class suburbia. We need to totally rethink and re-focus our ministries to serve the least of the sisters and brothers of Jesus first. Yes, we can serve the rich, but we must serve the poor and oppressed first. Who are these people? Where do they live? For the most part, most denominations don't seem to know even though the answers are at their doorsteps. We seem to want to keep the church's mission to the oppressed comfortably overseas. It seems to me the poor and oppressed on our own doorstep must be our starting point for planning for the turn of the century.

The fire is nearly burned down. The fall evening is all but spent. A year is nearly over, a decade soon passed by, a century all but consumed and a change in the millennium will soon be playing havoc with our computers. It is good to know that some things never change. Tomorrow, like Peter on that first day of resurrection following his threefold denial of Christ and accompanied by an exultation of roosters, I get another chance at being a faithful follower of my Lord. And so do you. ⌒

References

1. Marshall, Peter. 1950. By Invitation of Jesus. In *Mr. Jones Meet The Master: Sermons and Prayers of Peter Marshall,* New York, N.Y. Fleming H. Revell Co., p. 128.

2. Vinay, Tullio. Quoted in *Eerdmans' Handbook to Christian Belief,* (Wm.B.Eerdmans' Publishing Co., Grand Rapids, Michigan 1982), p. 397

Winter

REFLECTED LIGHT

It was 35 below and 2:00 in the morning. I parked the 4 x 4 in our yard and bowed my head to give thanks. I don't take the Lord's journey mercies lightly. They are my lifeline. As I slipped to the ground from behind the wheel of the truck, the snow squeaked loudly beneath my boots. I plugged the truck in for the night, grabbed a few things off of the seat and headed for the cozy warmth of the wood fire that I knew Linda would have burning in the house.

Something made me stop before seeking shelter. I turned and looked out to the lake. The sky was as clear and cold as bar ice. The moon was full and its reflected light illuminated the snow-covered lake as though it were mid-day. Earlier in the night near Pantage Lake, three hours to the north, I had turned my headlights off and driven for half a dozen miles using nothing but the reflected light from the moon. Now, as I stood looking out on the lake in front of our house in the same reflected light from the moon, I was tempted to go for my crosscountry skis just to enjoy the beauty and night brightness. I shook my head, smiled to myself, lifted the latch on the door and was swallowed by a gust of steam as I entered the house. Driver's fatigue and common sense had prevailed.

Reflected light from the moon. Isn't it amazing that a dark planetary body with no light of its own has the ability to totally illuminate our dark cold winter nights? Bill up at Nazko has told me that the solar panels with which he captures solar energy for his house can actually charge his storage batteries from the reflected light of the moon. The moon has no light of its own. It can only reflect light from the sun. And in our long, cold and dark nights the reflected light of the moon has the brightness to turn night almost into day.

We sinners are like that dark old cratered body in the sky. The Gospel of John talks about Jesus Christ as being the light of the world -- spiritual light that is -- who brings light into a world lost to the distortion and darkness of sin. Jesus tells his followers to be a light in the world. The problem is that we have no light in ourselves. Like the moon, we can only reflect light from the son: the Son of God, that is. And yet reflected light has the power to dispel cold darkness and illuminate the night in a profound and beautiful way.

From Under a Blazing Aspen

WINTER SPECULATION

It is winter! The night is endless, black and frigid. Our cottage-like living room is wood-fire warm and aglow with the soft light of a lamp on the oak whiskey barrel that serves as an end table. Nearby, an overstuffed couch has been trying to swallow me all evening, to the tunes of Loreena McKennitt. Snoozing normally comes easily to such a setting. Not tonight, at least not for me. Since the time of Descartes, it seems that quiet cold nights near a cozy wood fire were made for speculation. And so speculation enters the land of snooze in the person of my 3 ½ year old daughter Chelsea.

"Whatcha doin', Daddy?"

"Urmmmmph, snort, chortle, whaaa!?"

"I said, whatcha doin'?"

"Cough, snort, wheeze... Oh, mothly wakin' up, I gueth."

I grope around for my false teeth, which somehow have found their way into the longhaired rug beside the couch. Chelsea wiggles up on the couch and sits on my chest where her speculations will be impossible to ignore.

"What happened to your teeth, Daddy?"

"Some mean ole dentist pulled them out when I was 12."

"Why do dentists always pull out teeth?"

"'Cause it makes them rich, I guess."

"Why do they want to be rich anyway?"

"So they won't die poor."

"When you die, what happens to your money?"

"The people who bury you get it, I guess."

"When they bury you, what happens to your body?"

"I guess it (yawn) sort of soaks back into the dirt."

There is a long pause during which I almost succeed in drifting back to the land of snooze. The pause is then shattered with a timidly whispered question. "But Daddy, if our body is all soaked back into the dirt, what is Jesus going to do?"

Some questions from a three-year-old cut you right to the quick. Struggling to free myself from the clutches of the overstuffed couch, I sit up to try and address my little girl's speculation.

From Under a Blazing Aspen

"What is Jesus going to do" about the resurrection? I have to admit I tend to be like the people Paul must have been writing to in Corinth. I don't have a problem accepting that my soul is immortal but the very idea of a raised body is a mindbender. If my body is soaked back into the dust of creation upon my death, how can it be raised? If my body will be raised what will it look like? Will it look like it did in death? Oh perish the thought. If I am bone-honest with myself, my little girl's question is my question too. I can't answer her, I can only ask her question with her.

The Apostle Paul seems to have an answer for both of us. It is a mystery predicated on what he considers to be fact: the resurrection of Jesus Christ. He says, "Lo! I tell you a mystery...we shall all be changed..."(1Cor.15:51). Changed, from what is sown in the earth to a body chosen by God, from perishable to imperishable, from dishonour to glory, from terrestrial to celestial, from physical to spiritual, from mortal to immortal. Whatever else bodily resurrection means, at the very least it means unlimited transformation, a new creation.

I can't tell this to Chelsea! It is so full of words and theology. For me it raises as many questions as it answers. On one level this is good but on another level, the level of peering into one's own grave, Chelsea and I need something easier to cling to. John's answer to our question is the one that speaks to us most.

> "Beloved, we are children of God now; it does not yet appear what we shall be, but we know that when he appears we shall be like him" (1Jn.3:2).

What is Jesus going to do about the resurrection? Whatever it is, however he does it, whenever he comes, Chelsea, me and you will be raised from the dead and we will share in his risen nature. We will finally and completely be Christ-like. We will be a new creation with Jesus in the new creation of his completed Kingdom. Old things will have passed away. Oh blessed faith, hope and love!

SOMETHING OLD, SOMETHING NEW, SOME-THING BORROWED, SOMETHING BLUE

i. INTRODUCTION

It's midnight Wednesday. The air is brittle cold, the moon is full, the stars are bright and the Northern Lights are swirling above the silhouetted treetops on the horizon. Linda is sitting silently beside our sleeping 4-year-old daughter, Chelsea. The cab of the pickup is full of private thoughts as the diesel engine drones its way homeward. Mine are of the house church gathering that we shared a couple of hours ago.

We had been in a farmhouse 80 km from the nearest city, Prince George. The farmhouse was filled with people, almost half of them children. People gathered, talking about winter feeding of cattle and logging. Soon we were all sitting in a circle in the propane-lit living room, our thoughts turning to worship and prayer.

When the time was right, I read a psalm to bring our minds and hearts into unison before Christ. The guitar began to play and praise to God flowed effortlessly as everyone joined their lives and voices in Christian community. One person prayed for us and we all said the Lord's Prayer together. I remembered hearing one of the youngest children uttering the prayer. Someone chose a song. We sang it with gusto. Someone shared a thought and we were all blessed by it. One of the children picked out a chorus and everyone joined in the actions. Another child chose a chorus that got everyone clapping their hands and laughing. One of the grandparents selected a favourite old hymn and the children sang it with as much enthusiasm as any adult in the room.

As worship progressed, we prayed for Christ to dwell among us as we read the Word of God. Everyone had a try at reciting the memory verse from last week, with the children outdoing the adults as usual. Then the Scriptures for the night were read, each child reading a verse or two with parents helping the little ones as necessary. The children gathered at my feet, sitting cross-legged on the floor around me. I told a story sermon about Clodhopper the ugly horse and the time he broke wind and saved Sally from drowning. Everyone laughed. And then I talked about how physical appearances and irritating mannerisms were not roadblocks to the love of God or to the service of God -- how even the Apostle Paul was not perfect in appearance, health or mannerisms and yet he knew God's love and served Christ with his life. Laughter turned to contemplation.

Linda handed out church school curriculum to the younger children to complete on the floor in front of us while the older ones sat in the circle with the adults to enter into another task with Scripture. One person read another passage of Scripture and I spoke for a while

From Under a Blazing Aspen

about some points to keep in mind as we talked about it. After this we all had a chance to offer our insights into how the passage applied to our lives. The Word was proclaimed by the gathered community.

Gradually we shifted from sharing Scripture to sharing what was going on in our lives and in the life of the ranching community where we were. This flowed naturally into sharing the offering and prayers of the people, in which everyone of all ages took part. Some of the youngest prayed for the safety of their parents in their work and for farm animals that were sick. Some of the adults prayed for social issues. Someone prayed for peace in Bosnia and for the people of the other house churches that existed several hundred kilometers away in other parts of the Cariboo. We then gathered around the kitchen table where prayers of communion were said, the bread was broken and the wine shared. A verse of *Amazing Grace* was sung as we stood around the table of Our Lord, and the peace was passed. Later, tea, Kool-aid and cake were consumed as people continued to share their lives. Four hours after our arrival we crawled back into the frigid pickup and began our homeward journey.

In the icy bright night, driving through the aurora borealis, there is much reflection. In the light of tonight's reflection I am smiling. What a neat way to be the body of Christ and to share in the grace inherent in the fellowship of His body. I think of the children praying during prayer time, of how each person was free to fully participate in every aspect of worship, of the joy inherent in the choruses and hymns we sang, of the simplicity and authenticity. And I think about the risen Christ, present and smiling too. I think about the image of the church as bride of Christ in the Revelation of John. This night, I feel the joy of being part of the Lord's bride. I remember the several other house churches that make up the Cariboo Presbyterian Church congregation, how each of them in its own unique way is also so very precious and exciting; how they too are part of the bride of Christ in this rural ministry.

I reflect more on the bride image and an old saying comes to mind. It is one concerning brides and what they wear: "something old, something new, something borrowed, something blue". This night the old saying, in some queer way, seems to crystallize in my mind what we are about in this unique and exciting rural ministry. This night, in my mind, I begin to write an article that the *Presbyterian Record* has requested concerning this ministry.

ii. SOMETHING OLD

I have a friend in the country who loves sports cars. He is particularly fond of a product from the city of Milan in Italy. He insists it is fun to own and exciting to operate. He also spends most of his money and spare time monkey-wrenching the thing, trying to keep it on the road (the closest dealership is 200 miles away in the nearest large city). In my opinion, this mechanical marvel from Milan is not a car for the country. It is too costly to maintain, and impractical. A pickup truck is a lot more effective. A pickup is much closer to what old Henry Ford had in mind when he built the first production automobile, designed to be practical and affordable to the pedestrian person.

The Christian church as most of us know it today is also a product of Milan. Many years ago Emperor Constantine, with his famous Edict of Milan, pronounced freedom of worship for all Christians (313 AD). This resulted in basilicas springing up to replace the house church which had been the Christian norm for the first two and a half centuries of its often-persecuted existence. Since the Edict of Milan the church has become, for the main part, building-oriented. Elaborate buildings with highly developed programs and liturgies are products of Milan. They have become the norm for the church. As such, the church is fun to own and exciting to operate -- sort of like a racy Italian sports car. It is also highly expensive and not very practical for rural areas. In rural areas like those in the Cariboo, we need a church that more closely resembles a pickup. A church closer to the first model. A church that is practical and affordable.

For us in the Cariboo, a church more closely resembling a pickup is powered by an understanding of church which insists Christian community gathered around the Word and Sacrament are the norm, not an elaborate building and its associated trappings. As the first two and a half centuries of church history and a few contemporary models of house church prove, people can experience the healing love of Christ in a powerful way by gathering in small worship groups in family homes. These gatherings seem to be richest if they are totally inclusive of adults and children. And so the bride of Christ in the Cariboo chose the ancient house church model as its "something old".

iii. SOMETHING NEW

In using something old you have to make it new, or at least make it contemporary. In this regional rural house church expression of the bride of Christ, "something new" has often been just a new twist. For example, it is a new twist for our denomination to begin a ministry with the congregational vision intentionally and permanently excluding a church building. We are committed to the house church model as our congregational vision. This frees the congregation to focus totally on people instead of on church facilities and the stuff of institution. So our model is old but our vision for using it in the Presbyterian Church in Canada brings a new twist in emphasis for church extension.

Another new approach used in our ministry is the idea of a regional congregation. I suppose this is really just a new twist on the old multi-point charges that we maintain in so many rural areas. However, multi-point charges are really multi-congregation ministries. Our many house churches are all part of one congregation. This results in significant differences, which include:

a) No multi-buildings owned and maintained by the multi-congregations.

b) No running to three or more church services on a Sunday. Our house church services are spread throughout the region throughout the week.

c) No separate Session and Board for each point of ministry. We function with one central Session which meets quarterly. We have no permanent boards or committees.

Recently our congregation gave another new spin to an old idea. Presbyterians have had multi-staff ministries for years. They are almost exclusively an urban-suburban phenomenon in our denomination. They are also normally set up with a senior pastor and one or more junior pastors. A truly associate team ministry with all members of the team being equal in terms of responsibility and function seldom seems to work in our denomination. In 1994 our regional rural house church congregation went to a full associate team ministry when we called Shannon Bell-Wyminga and John Wyminga to join me in ordained ministry. It is working beautifully. We have a team ministry plan that took four months to develop and it has been ratified by the whole congregation. We don't get to see one another as often as we would like, for the Cariboo region is a large piece of ground and there is so much work to do. We are, however, committed as a team to meet weekly for brainstorming and prayer. This team approach to rural ministry has already blessed us in many ways.

Some of our "something new" is not just a new twist. Normally when our denomination has started a new work there is much worrying and fussing about Presbyterian distinctives and bringing a Presbyterian witness into a community. Normally, in church extension work, we invite all people to our church but our goal is to turn them into Presbyterians as soon as possible. Ecumenism is left as a concept for inter-church dialogue. In the Cariboo ministry we don't talk about ecumenism -- we are fiercely committed to it as a way of life. Denominationalism is an urban-suburban luxury that has no place in our rural ministry. There are not enough of us to denominate. And so the house churches are made up of people from every denomination under the Son. No person is ever pressured to become Presbyterian. Every person is encouraged to contribute from his or her own tradition to the life of the congregation. This has sometimes left us struggling with church polity, but when this has happened we work in the spirit of the reformers and err on the side of grace. I find this distinctly new and different, even from the interdenominational "shared ministries" that we have historically been involved with in more remote areas.

iv. SOMETHING BORROWED

I wish I could claim credit for the idea of running all over the Cariboo facilitating house churches in rural areas. The truth of the matter is that as bride of Christ in the Cariboo we have incorporated the idea as "something borrowed". If you are of the type that likes to browse through old church records, and if you look up the statistics for the Presbyterian Synod of BC for 1925, what you will find is this. The Rev. Dr. A.D. McKinnon was the Presbyterian minister serving the south half of the Cariboo. He worked out of Williams Lake, which was a small cow town at that time. His area went from Clinton in the south to McLeese Lake in the north (about 300 km) and from Alexis Creek in the west to Horsefly and Bridge Lake in the east (about 200 km). Although this is somewhat smaller than the area served by the Cariboo Presbyterian Church today, much of the travel had to be done by wagon trail and I assume on horse back. At that time, to the best of my knowledge, there were two tiny church buildings and 20 preaching stations, the latter similar to our house churches. Dr. McKinnon had a total of 1200 rural people under his pastoral care with 200 children in Sunday school. Dr. McKinnon stayed in this work for several years. I still find oldtimers here who remember his ministry. He was much loved and he must have loved what he was doing with a passion. I think I know how he felt.

If you think this is an anomaly for the 1925 period, look one valley to the west and you will find the Rev. D.K. Faris serving an area from Kamloops in the south to Blue River in the north (about 300 km). He had 30 preaching stations, 1000 under his pastoral care and 128 children. This is a story you will find repeated over and over again in the first quarter of this century in all of the major denominations as the church stretched itself to serve rural people in the west. My great-grandfather, the Rev. Charles Webber, a Methodist minister, carried on a similar ministry at the turn of the century on the west coast of BC. He travelled by boat and his area went from Victoria in the south to the Alaska border in the north. His parishioners numbered in the hundreds and were all rural folks.

One of the things this kind of ministry necessitated was the use of what we call "house church mentors" and what they called "lay preachers". There was no way that one minister could be everywhere every week. At that time, our denomination had a book of services especially for lay preachers to use in the ministry of supporting the work of the ordained minister. The idea of the gifts of the whole people of God was taken very seriously then. It is something we are borrowing and using as we choose and train mentors from house churches to augment ordained ministry.

So you see, the idea of a regional rural ministry with well-qualified pastors and non-ordained assistants or mentors serving rural pastorates hundreds of kilometers across with up to 20 or 30 points of ministry is a borrowed idea from our past. It works as well today as it did then.

v. SOMETHING BLUE

The bride of Christ in the Cariboo chose as "something blue" something Presbyterian. This totally ecumenical work is totally funded and supported by the Presbyterian Church in Canada. The Presbytery of Kamloops adopted our vision for rural missions in 1988. At first there was no funding available from the national Church budget so people and congregations in the Synod of BC were challenged to raise funds to support the beginning of this ministry. In the fall of 1989, the Cariboo Presbyterian Church was officially established as a regional rural house church congregation totally funded by the Synod of BC. Today, this ministry still receives approximately 40% of its funding directly from gifts and bequests from people and churches in the Synod of BC, and others. Approximately 40% of the funding comes from national church's mission funds and the rest is raised locally.

The polity of the congregation is also totally Presbyterian. As mentioned earlier, the congregation of many house churches functions as one church. It has one Session (elders' board), one set of books and is under the pastoral care of one Presbytery. We function as any other Presbyterian church does in terms of church government. Presbyterian polity is a real gift when it comes to caring for a unique and different congregation such as ours in the Cariboo.

vi. CONCLUSION

One of my associates, John, tells of a time when he was coming home late at night from a house church gathering somewhere in the Cariboo. He parked the 4 x 4 in front of his house and extracted himself from it. He paused and looked up at the starlit sky. He smiled and shook his head, saying; "...and they actually pay me to do this?" I guess that sort of sums it up for me too. Rural ministry in the Cariboo is hard and often hazardous work, with the many hours we spend driving on less-than-perfect roads. It is also extremely enjoyable. The people and the country make it that way. ⌒

ARE ANGELS ALL WE NEED?

"While he was going and they were gazing up toward heaven, suddenly two men in white robes stood by them. They said, "Men of Galilee, why do you stand looking up toward heaven? This Jesus, who has been taken up from you into heaven, will come in the same way as you saw him go into heaven." (Acts 1:10-11).

When I was a kid, I used to like to pull tricks on adults. I discovered if you wanted to trick an adult, particularly one who had been tricked before, you had to take advantage of naturally-occurring human tendencies embedded deep within the subconscious. If you did this properly, an individual was rendered absolutely helpless and seemingly as dumb as a sack of hammers. In such a state, tricking them was plumb easy.

This hobby required that I spend a fair bit of time observing adult human behaviour to determine these naturally-occurring human tendencies. I had the perfect laboratory for such observations. I grew up in a lumber camp and had the run of the mill, so to speak. The men of the mill never knew it, but they were my human guinea pigs. I observed their tendencies: to tell unbelievable stories and begin to believe them themselves, to massage their own egos at the expense of others and to look like they were busy while doing nothing. One particular tendency was noted at the back of the planer shed where the men would often go to expel the coffee consumed liberally at smoke time. The men would stand and stare off into space with the most vacant look imaginable on their faces as they relieved themselves, some for unbelievably long periods of time.

Closer observation revealed that this habit of staring off into space was often practiced at other times as well. Quite regularly, when the foreman wasn't looking, I would catch one of the lumbermen with his hands thrust deep into his pockets, staring off into nowhere with an expression of vacancy etched on his face. They could hold this pose for a surprisingly long time if the foreman was not around.

One day I decided to try out my latest observations in a trick. The goal was to trick as many adults as possible in a short period of time. Most of the men at the mill had been deceived so many times that they had become totally gun-shy and as a result were not the best candidates for any more trickery. So, one fine 24th of May my friend Billy and I positioned ourselves just off the country road that ran by our house.

Cars came speeding down the road, intently piloted by long weekend holiday types. Billy and I positioned ourselves just off the edge of the road. We stood staring off into space, vacant looks on our faces and our hands shading our eyes. One of the first drivers to come by tried to look up to see what we were staring at. He neither stopped nor otherwise slowed down the car. He careened off the pavement and created quite a show sliding about on the gravel shoulder before regaining control and embarrassedly speeding on his way. Other drivers and their passengers similarly looked up, some slowing down considerably and putting their heads right out the window to see what the two boys were staring at.

Things were going along just fine until a big black Lincoln came along. The car screeched to a halt; an old man about five feet tall got out from behind the wheel and proceeded to stare vacantly off into space to see what the dickens we were looking at. After about a minute he realized he had been had. Without a word to us he turned towards the car with the words, "Get 'em, Bud!" Before we realized what was happening, the largest doberman pinscher God ever dreamed of constructing bailed over the front seat of the Lincoln and bore down on us like a seriously-perturbed rodeo bull.

We wanted to run, honest to God we did, but we were both too busy looking off into space with vacant stares on our faces and relieving ourselves, lumberjack fashion, in our pants. Bud ran up to us, sniffed us, growled, turned and strutted back to the car. He and the little old man flashed an impish grin at one another as they popped back into the car and accelerated slowly down the road. We decided we had best get on with something a little more productive and a little less dangerous. We walked off as nonchalantly as you can with shaking knees in wet pants.

This childhood memory reminds me of the first 11 verses of the book of Acts. In this passage, we are told first that Jesus presented himself as raised from the grave, by many convincing proofs, over a period of 40 days after his resurrection. Secondly, during this 40 day period, Jesus taught the disciples about the Kingdom of God. Thirdly, before His ascension he gave them several explicit instructions regarding what they were to do when he was taken up to God. This included:

   i) go to Jerusalem;

   ii) receive the Holy Spirit;

   iii) forget about your own agendas, such as the restoration of the Kingdom to Israel;

   iv) instead of your own agenda you have one task and only one: to bear witness to the risen Christ, in Jerusalem, in all of Judea, in neighboring Samaria, and to the ends of the earth.

Seems pretty clear to me as I read it. A few simple instructions and one explicit command. That one explicit command was to bear witness to the resurrection. As I read more of the book of Acts I find that whatever else the Church is doing, it must always do one thing: bear witness to the resurrected Lord, who is Lord of all the earth. In the Acts account, Jesus is taken up to sit at the right hand of God where he will remain as the Lord of all the earth. He has been gone for just minutes. And there they are, those early disciples, *staring off into space,* seemingly with vacant looks on their faces.

It is a natural human tendency, this staring off into space. It is related to other natural human tendencies like twiddling one's thumbs and other forms of whiling away the time. The disciples of Jesus seemed particularly prone to various forms of consuming time. They fell asleep when Jesus asked them to watch out for him while he prayed. They packed up and went off fishing when they should have been giving witness to the resurrection of Jesus. Jesus said of them, "The spirit is willing but the flesh is weak." When the boss was not around, they were as like as not to find some way of idling away the time. That is exactly what happened the first day they were left alone, as recounted in Acts, chapter one.

I am tempted to think that I make too big a thing of this standing around and staring off into space. Standing around doing nothing is not that big a deal. The disciples will get around to it eventually. But if it is not such a big deal, why the angels in this story? We are not talking just one, either. We are talking two angels, who show up "immediately". Jesus has been gone from his disciples for about a minute and he has to send two angels dressed in white to act as his foremen and to say, "Quit standing around staring off into space and doing nothing. Get on with doing what he told you to do two minutes ago."

Boy, am I glad we are not as prone to standing around and doing nothing as those early disciples were. When I read my Bible I get a glimpse of the early church. In the book of Acts I see texts like Chapter 2 which says:

> "They devoted themselves to the apostles' teaching and fellowship, to the breaking of bread and the prayers."
> (Acts 2:42)

That's what the church is to be about I say: teaching, fellowship, worship, sharing and praying. And so that's what I do, and I do a good job of it too. It's good and important work.

I am going to write myself out onto a limb here. I think that this is not what the church is supposed to be doing...JUST! And if that's all I am doing it amounts to standing around and doing nothing. What Jesus said we all should be doing is very simple. "In the power of the Holy Spirit, we are to be his witnesses...witnesses to the Risen Christ and to his lordship of all the earth... to all the Earth." *That is our main job as Christian persons. That is our main job as a Christian church.*

The Apostle puts it even more clearly when he states that God has put all things under the feet of the risen Christ and has made him head over all things for the church, "...which is his body, the fullness of him who fills all in all" (Eph.1:23). The church is the fullness of Christ in the world. I don't see anywhere that it says it is to be a mute silent fullness in the world. We are to be witnesses. And if anyone can tell me how you and I can be effective witnesses without getting outside of the church and talking about Jesus, I am listening.

And I say, "But I am not good with words." And Christ says, "That's why you have the Holy Spirit....which I promised will give you the utterance." And I say, "But first we need a couple of angels."

Is that what we need, you and I? A couple of angels, Christ's foremen, to come down and say, "What on earth are you standing around gawking for? Get on with it"? I think maybe a couple of angels with a doberman named Bud might be effective. It just might stop us from gawking off into space in reverent inactivity. You know what? If we did get on with this witnessing to the resurrection of Christ to people outside the church, our churches would be overflowing with people. Instead we hire professional evangelists and preachers and invent all kinds of ways to get around doing what it is we are supposed to be doing ourselves. Again, we the people remain prone to standing around doing something other than what we are called to do. When will we ever learn? "Hey Bud! Come here, boy!" ⌢

TENDING TO THE HEART SPRINGS

He was home. It was Christmas Day. He was not happy. Exactly why he was not feeling at all joyful or for that matter even peaceful was a troublesome mystery to him. After all, he had done the right things: travelled home for the first time in ten years to be with his parents, gone Christmas shopping to purchase special gifts, participated in the decorating of the old family farmhouse, gone visiting old family friends with his parents. Why, he had even gone out with some of his buddies from childhood days to some of the old Christmas haunts to see if he could stir up a spirit from Christmas past. And after all that, he still felt blah. Actually, he didn't really feel anything. And that sent the cold iron of fear deep within his soul. It had turned out to be a rather foul Christmas for him.

Christmas was not all that was foul. The family drinking water stunk too. He was looking forward to a long cool drink of spring water from the taps of the old family farmhouse. Ten years in the big city drinking chlorinated and fluoridated soup had left him with a deep thirst for a large, cold, unadulterated glass of spring water. In fact, it was the first thing he did when he opened the door to the old farmhouse. He went for the tap even before he hugged his parents. He turned it on and let it run till it was cold…filled a large tumbler…lifted it to his lips to guzzle its refreshing contents down. And then he caught the smell. A moment later he also caught the taste, the smell and taste of rotting vegetation. "What in hell is wrong with the water?", he yelled out to his parents.

They did not have to answer. He suddenly noticed they were both very old. His Mom's hands were gnarled with crippling arthritis. His Dad was hunched over with the pain of an old farm accident that left him barely able to walk with a cane. So late Christmas Day found him hiking alone up the steep hill to the spring that fed water to the family home. He remembered how this walk had been a ritual for him and his father every Sunday after church. Before supper they would walk up the steep trail, talking and sometimes laughing about the things that had filled their lives in the past week. Eventually they would come to the bubbling spring and its crystal pool of wonderful water. Here they paused, both sitting silently for a time enjoying the solitude of that place. It was prayer in its deepest sense. Then after some time father and son would silently stoop and remove the leaves and grass and twigs that had fallen into the pool of the spring. And the water always remained cool, clear and sweet.

Now, slow-footed through the snow that covered the steep trail, he made his way alone to the spring. As he arrived at the old familiar pool he was shocked at what he found. Rotting leaves, fallen trees, dead grass and old fir branches covered with green slime. The water, once clear, was now brown. The water, once sweet, was now putrid. The same water from the same source no longer brought the same satisfaction, refreshment or renewal. How long has it been

From Under a Blazing Aspen

since Dad has been too old to climb up here to maintain the spring, he wondered.

He stooped and began to pull things from the water. First the rotting trees, then the decaying branches, and finally, after much effort to locate the old rake that was kept hanging in a nearby tree, he raked out all the leaves. He cleaned the screen over the end of the pipe that fed water from the bottom of the pool to the taps of the farmhouse two kilometers below. Then he sat in the wet snow at the edge of the spring and listened to the bubbling water flow over the little board catchment dam that backed the water up to form the pool.

Time passed and he lost himself in quiet thought. Actually it was more like quiet questioning. Why? Why was this Christmas such a bummer? Why were all the Christmases of the past ten years such bummers? Why had most of his life become a bummer? He reflected that most of what he experienced in the past ten years, both the good things and the not so good, had not brought him much peace or edification. Life had become sour, foul, broken. He'd thought coming home for Christmas would somehow solve all that, that the old memories of peace and joy that were so much a part of his past life at home with his parents would be waiting there for him. They had not waited there for him.

He closed his eyes and sat in silence for what seemed like an eternity. Finally in desperation he whispered a simple prayer: "Oh, Christ of Christmas, help me." A strangely familiar silent voice deep in his being responded.

He opened eyes wet with tears to look at the water that was even now beginning to clear. As he watched, he became aware that somehow the absence of peace and grace was in some strange way like the fouled spring. The peace he had once known as an integral part of his life, the grace he had known as a way of being, had somehow gotten polluted, fouled, putrefied, distorted. Could it be, could it be that simple? Could it be that the grace of the Christ of Christmas was always there? Could it be that the peace of Christ was always there, just like the spring water was always there? Could it be, like the spring water that needed regular tending in order to receive its full freshness and sweet taste, that the grace and peace of Christ also needed to be tended regularly in order to receive the full power of them in one's life?

He began to remember the Christmas story he had heard read in church that very morning. It had not meant much to him when the old priest had read it. But now, as he thought about it beside the spring, some of the characters in that ancient story became significant. Angels, shepherds, Joseph, Mary, all tending to the Christ in their own way, each receiving the Christ and his unadulterated peace and grace into their lives, leaving them singing with joy or pondering joy in their hearts. By memory he thought of others from that story: Elizabeth, Zechari'ah, the Magi, Simeon and the prophetess Anna. Again, all tending to the Christ of Christmas in their own way, each receiving the Christ Child and the fullness of his peace and grace. And he thought about his childhood with his parents and how they taught him to tend to the grace and peace of Christ. How they took him to church for hymns and sermons, read Scripture expectantly, prayed regularly, spent time in quiet solitude with Christ. For the first time he became aware that all of these things were like pulling the fallen vegetation out of the spring so its purity and freshness could grace life. He also became acutely aware that this Christ and grace-tending had somehow fallen out of his life when he had left home ten years ago.

There, on the bank of the now crystal-clear pool of spring water, he was converted again to the grace of Christ and to a life of discipleship tending to that grace. He said softly, " Oh Christ, I give you my life anew this Christmas, I come to you." Surprised by the love of God for the first time in ten years, he wept quietly but joyfully, as in his own way he stood with Mary, Joseph, the shepherds, the Magi, Elizabeth, Zachari'ah, Simeon and Anna to receive the Christ of Christmas and his peace that passeth all understanding. And he was filled with a strange familiar quiet warmth deep within.

He reached down and took a handful of the cool, fresh, clear spring water as though to drink it. Instead he uttered the ancient Latin words of baptism: "...*et nominae Patri, et Filis, et Spiritus Sanctus*..." and poured the water over his head. "Merry Christmas," he whispered to himself.

CHRISTMAS STALKING

"I don't think I like this. Let's get the dickens out of here!" Linda said in an alarmed whisper.

We had been out on snowshoes all day. The snow was at least five feet deep in the mountain pass and we had been taking turns breaking trail. Our journey had taken us up an old wagon trail for several miles. Once there, we had lit a small fire to toast our cheese sandwiches and make a billycan full of sweet tea. Now we were returning on the same trail. The going was quite easy since it was well beaten down from our trip in. The bush was beautiful and filled with the silence and solitude that only isolation and heavy snow cover can furnish. That is why I was so surprised at the alarm in Linda's voice when she spoke.

"That darn cat has been following us all day," she said. "And he is a big one too."

We both knelt down on the fronts of our Trapper-Nelson snowshoes and closely examined the fresh cougar tracks in the middle of the snowshoe trail we had made in the morning. They were almost five inches wide in the packed snow of the trail, ranking this particular cougar as a large specimen in anyone's record book. The tracks were not very far apart, irregular and deliberate, which indicated that the cougar was moving very slowly. It had moved off the trail when it had heard us returning, floundering through the snow and into a thicket of young fir trees. It was quite likely watching us as we spoke.

"Do you think he is hungry, curious or just using our snowshoe trail for easy passage?" queried Linda, still speaking in a whisper.

"I don't know for sure if he is curious or hungry," I said. "As far as I am concerned, it doesn't really matter. From what I know about cougars, the way this fella's tracks are so irregular and yet deliberate indicates that he is probably stalking us. If he is stalking us, it kind of rules out the easy passage theory, doesn't it? I think it's time we made an exit!"

I spoke with all the calmness I could gather. I certainly wasn't feeling that way. I was wishing I had bought my rifle with us, or even our Airedale who was well known for putting the run on anything, including large bears. But I had not, and now there was nothing to do but to snowshoe back towards our 4 x 4 pickup, showing as much boldness and bravado as our meager acting abilities could muster. And that is exactly what we did, thankfully, without a courtesy call from Tom Cougar.

This cougar experience happened several years ago, in the bush near the summit of the Blueberry Pass, in southern BC. It has left a lasting impression on me about the nature of cougars and their habit of deliberate stalking. If you have ever watched the family cat after a mouse in the tall grass at the edge of your lawn, you know what I mean by "deliberate stalking". Each stalking movement is slow, calculated and completely focussed on obtaining what is being hunted. To the cat family, while they are stalking nothing else exists. Every movement and thought is completely dedicated to the stalk -- and to what is being stalked.

As I make my preparations this Advent for the Christmas season, this image of deliberate stalking from nature is lodged in my mind, along with a Christmas dilemma. This season is all about peace. For Christians, it is a particular kind of peace. It is the peace of Christ. Christ said to his followers:

> "Peace I leave with you; my peace I give to you; not as the world gives do I give to you. Let not your hearts be troubled, neither let them be afraid"(Jn.14:27 RSV).

And yet, every Christmas, and more times throughout the year than I like to admit, the peace of Christ seems to elude me.

Particularly at Christmas my life seems to become frantic and fractured. There are a thousand things to do and less than half enough time to do them in. Every Christmas finds me whipping myself into a seasonal lather of busyness. It affects every aspect of my life, work and family. Each year I sing the same lament: "Oh, I just can't seem to get into the Christmas spirit this year." What is missing as Christmas spirit is the experience of the peace of Christ that the world cannot give or understand. I know this mystical peace at other times in the year, but hardly ever at Christmas.

It strikes me that inherent in the giving of something is the receiving. Christ gives His peace, that is the Biblical promise. But I wonder how I go about receiving it at Christmas? Do I just go about life and wait for it to surprise me on some wintry street corner, perhaps as I take a second or two to gaze at the seasonal display of lights, and for a nanosecond enjoy its nurture? This hardly seems to me to be adequate.

This year it comes to my mind that perhaps that big cat on the Blueberry Pass and my experience of being stalked has some discipleship to teach me. Could it be that the peace that so eludes me at Christmas needs stalking? What I mean by this is, perhaps I need to become intentional about the peace of Christ, particularly at busy times like Christmas. Perhaps I need to stalk peace in the same slow, calculated, deliberate and focussed fashion as Tom Cougar stalked Linda and me in that snowy pass so many years ago. As to peace, perhaps I need to become like that big cat is to prey: while he is stalking, nothing else exists, every movement and thought completely dedicated to the stalk, and to that which is being stalked. My sense is that if I approach the peace of Christ this way, I stand a much better chance of availing myself of it.

If I look at this whole question of stalking Christmas peace, or for that matter, peace at any time of the year, through the binoculars of history, I find that what I am thinking about is borne out in the history of Christian spirituality. From Jesus to the Apostles, to the Desert Fathers, to the monastic Brothers, to the early Reformers, to the Puritans and Quakers, there is a constant thread of stalking peace through the Christian discipline of contemplative prayer. Contemplative prayer is nothing more or less than slowly, deliberately, intentionally and completely focusing on Christ. This is not the worrying in front of God that many of my fleeting prayers have become. Rather it is the kind of prayer born out of solitude, silence and meditation. It is the kind of prayer where God is the focus, not myself or anyone or anything. It is prayer for God's sake, not mine. It is prayer that seeks to place oneself in the exclusive presence of God for God to do with as God wills. It is prayer that listens much and speaks little. It is the kind of prayer that the likes of Thomas Akempis, Brother Lawrence, Dietrich Bonhoeffer, Thomas Merton, Henri Nouwen, Richard Foster and Eugene Peterson have written so profoundly about.

I have done it before, I must do it again. It is so easy to do, this stalking peace. For me it involves carving out time and place to be alone and silent. There, in my "prayer closet", I find a passage of Scripture, quite often from the Psalms, to help me focus. I ask Christ to be present to me as I read a verse or two over and over until I no longer need to read it, but can simply say it in my mind, over and over, until it becomes a part of me. After a time I sit in complete silence and when I feel as though I have somehow climbed upon the knee of God where I am but a wee child, I sit for Him there. There, I am free to speak as a child to a completely loving parent, to listen or just to be silent. And then when the time is right, usually after a half hour or so, I thank God and slowly return to what He has placed in my day for me. I take this time spent with God and for God into the day with me, often pausing to once again thank Him. And somehow, the peace of Christ that the world cannot understand seeps into the moment and even the day.

This Advent, in the light of memories of snowy days and cougars stalking, in the sensing of my present darkness and the need to experience of the peace of Christ at Christmas, I am going to be Christmas stalking.

The peace of Christ be with you!

GOAT SHADOWS

We used to live with mountain goats. Twenty eight years ago, while still in our first year of marriage, I took a job as a lookout man with the British Columbia Forest Service (there were no lookout women in those days). My posting was Grave Mountain lookout, just a few mile south of Mt. Assiniboine in the Rocky Mountains of southeastern BC. This meant that Linda, our young Airedale Basil, our groceries and me were flown to a craggy mountaintop about 9000 feet above sea level, just a spit from the Continental Divide. There we were dropped off to live for three summer months in a cabin that was 14 feet square with wall-to-wall windows. A fire-finder, the tool of my new trade, took up the centre quarter of the floor space. Our single army cot took up the south wall. Linda and I shared it with Basil.

It would prove to be a time rich in memories. The most exciting thing about those three months, outside the frequent lightning storms blasting the top of the mountain, was watching the mountain goats. We had two maternal groups, each consisting of a dozen animals, and a couple of solitary old urine-stained males. Mountain goats seemed to be framed in one of our endless windows all summer long.

Most often, they were on some high and impossible snow-covered cliff, perched there like an out of place ornament on the edge of some giant wedding cake. We got to know a lot about mountain goats that summer. It was like we became the closest of friends.

It was a friendship that we have not been able to renew these 28 years, until last summer. On a trip from Bella Coola, just before ascending the infamous Hill, we rounded a corner and just about ran over four mountain goats with our 4 x 4.

"What on earth are those stupid goats doing down here?" I yelled, as I braked furiously and swerved to miss the two nannies and their kids. "Mountain goats are supposed to have the good sense to live on the safety of some 1000 foot cliff, not in the middle of a lush and populated coastal valley. They could get killed down here."

"Could be that they are on holidays just like us," said Linda. "Oh look! I haven't seen such cute little kids since the Lookout. Quick, get out and take a picture."

"Do you think I am totally insane?" I said, as I jammed the gears into reverse and began to back up to where the goats were licking the rocks on the side of the road. "I know an old trapper who got caught doing the close quarter shuffle with a couple mountain goats on the edge of a cliff. His faithful companion dog was skewered by the razor-sharp horns of a nanny who got a little overzealous with her baby-sitting. She planted her horns right through Rover's heart and then proceeded to take a bead on the old trapper, who was in the midst of beating his tail down the mountain. If it wasn't for his faithful dog earning him a good head start, he would have had his

From Under a Blazing Aspen

rear anatomy permanently altered. I ain't about to expose my best side to an irked mother goat and send some proctologist to the Caribbean as a result."

"Aw, they look so cute," said Linda. "We just have to get a couple of pictures. Roll your window down and I will get the camera ready. You can take the pictures from the safety of the truck. Make sure that you get at least one picture of the kids."

By now I was parked just opposite the two nannies and the kids, only a few meters away. I was trying to imagine what the truck would look like with a hole sliced through the door panel by goat horns. I slid over a foot from the door as I estimated the door's thickness to be about half the length of the goats' horns.

The nannies were nervous at the perceived threat to their young kids. They were also not about to run off and leave the salt they craved on the rocks at the side of the road. And so they went into deep defensive mode to provide maximum protection for their beloved babies.

"Quick, stupid, snap the picture, and don't you dare miss getting those darling little kids in it," encouraged Linda.

"I have already snapped three and each time I squeeze the trigger on the camera, the kids are not to be seen," I said. Those nannies place themselves right between the kids and us. It is like the kids are in a constant shadow of protection."

I backed the truck up a bit more to see if I could get a better angle. The nannies would have none of my tricks. They just moved their bodies around as I jockeyed for position and the kids were constantly in their shadow of protection. We sat and watched for a while longer. The kids got a little restless and began to move around themselves. For a moment I thought I might get a clear shot at them. However with each of the cherished ones' moves, or with each of our moves as the perceived predators and the source of danger, the nanny goats positioned themselves between us to cast a complete shadow of protection on the kids. I knew that the only way to get to those kids was over the dead bodies of the nannies. They would protect their babies to the very end by standing between them and any source of danger, casting a shadow of protection.

We continued our trip, winding up the 20 or more kilometers of 18% grade to the top of the Bella Coola hill (you have got to drive this thing to believe it. Words just cannot do it justice). The slow grinding trip gave me time to reflect upon what we had just experienced. As usual, when left to reflect, my mind usually finds its way to thinking about God stuff.

That was last summer. As I write, it is deep winter and the beginning of a new year, almost the beginning of a new millennium. The new year is always a time for me when I am faced with the unknown. To be frank, the unknown is not a comfortable place for me. I find that fear lives there and fear is not one of my favourite things. In the face of all this I find myself being drawn back to last summer's goat shadows and the subsequent thoughts I had about Scripture while driving up the Bella Coola hill.

There are many parts of the Bible that go right over my head until some experience with Nature presents itself to me. Nature's pulpit has always been the source of the best Biblical proclamation for me. And so it was with the goat shadows.

Psalms 17:8 and 91:1, along with Isaiah 49:2 and 51:16, all talk about finding protection in the shadow of God. The Biblical metaphor is meant to be rich in how it portrays God's protection, and yet for me the idea of a shadow is problematic. A shadow is a fleeting, almost ghost-like presence with no substance to it and which is only briefly perceived, if at all. I don't find comparing God's protection to a shadow all that comforting. I want to think of God's protection as being somewhat more substantial than a shadow.

Up to now I have thought of God's protective shadow as a bystander. I have looked at it from the side. But if I think of it from the perspective of a participant, either as a source of danger or as one being protected, the concept of shadow is powerful. From this perspective "the shadow of the Almighty" can only be perceived as God standing between that which he loves and that which seeks to harm. This never struck me until I looked at it from the perspective of being a predator to the goat kids and watching the nannies place themselves between me and their beloved. Being in the protective shadow of those nannies is something substantial.

Abiding in the shadow of the Almighty, or resting in the shadow of the hand of God, really means that God stands between me and the enemy. It means that God has pushed me behind him and stands forth willing to die for me. "Oh Christ, now I understand." Bring on the new year. Bring on the new millennium.

⟺ Spring ⟺

VANTAGE POINTS

One of my best friends, Halden, who also doubles as my son, was sitting in the front of the pickup as we were driving slowly and talking about fast cars. The topic had turned to pre-1969 Mustangs just as we rounded the bend to begin the descent down Rosebud Hill. In the middle of a debate on long block versus short block engines in older Mustangs, we lost the road. It had been converted into a good sized stream when the snowmelt decided the path of least resistance was right down the centre of the gravel road. A lovely babbling brook was carving out a very scenic canyon and we found ourselves parked right in the middle of this creative process. We were tempted to commence fly-fishing from the roof of the pickup, but we were late for house church. Halden locked in the hubs and we proceeded towards the Poole's ranch in four-wheel drive, navigating across several attractive lakes on the way. Spring can be an exciting adventure in the Cariboo -- from the vantage point of a pair of gum boots and a good 4 x 4.

It's an entirely different thing if you are meeting spring head on and trying to stop its overenthusiastic waters from flooding your home.

You sandbag, ditch, drain and pray yourself into complete exhaustion, often losing the battle in the end and getting weeks, if not months, of depressing cleanup work for your troubles. From the vantage point of a house that is being forced to act as a boat, spring is a terrifying experience of tears.

I have become increasingly sensitive of late to the significance of perspective when it comes to how one experiences life. Depending upon where you find yourself sitting at the time, spring flooding is either an adventure or a tragedy, - 48 degrees Celsius is either a delight to the senses or a life-threatening challenge, calving season is either a field filling with cuteness or an exhausting ritual of sleepless nights, building a new home is a catalyst for delightful dreams of new possibilities or a nightmare of neverending tasks. It all seems to depend upon one's vantage point.

Not many years ago I met a fellow who has the ability to place himself at vantage points from which life always appears positive. That is not to say that this fellow does not experience hard times because I know he often does. But he has that mystical ability of always finding something funny or good in the experience. If his house was swept away in a flood I expect he would be exuberant about the way the neighbours pitched in to help him save it and the coming adventure of building a new one. I am not always sure how to take him. Do I admire this fellow or do I let his eternal (at times pronounced "infernal" by me) optimism depress me? One thing is sure, he generates within me a powerful curiosity.

It was only a matter of time until I cornered this incorrigible optimist with questions. When I asked him the obvious, wouldn't you know it, his answer was in the form of a question, " 'Who do you believe in and what is your purpose in life?' I continually ask myself these two questions." I knew I had to gnaw on this one for a while. I exchanged niceties and quickly left. What follows is a rendered-down version of my gnawing on the theological bone my friend had thrown me.

When I face up to who I believe in, I face up to God, who is completely sovereign (or in complete control) over life in general and my life in particular. I face up to God, who is love, and expresses that love to all creation and to my life in particular. I face up to God, who has revealed his person, love and sovereignty in the person of Jesus Christ, who says to me,

> "In the world you have tribulation; but be of good cheer, I have overcome the world"(Jn.16:33 RSV).

If God is ultimately in control of all of life and my life in particular, and if God is love and loves me specifically, that kind of places me at a certain positive vantage point in life.

When I face up to my purpose in life, again I face up to God. Ultimately my purpose is to drink God's draught of life to the last drop and enjoy it fully. I suppose I have many purposes, but my prime purpose is to enjoy and glorify God, who is full of love for me and in control of my life. The only way I can figure how to live, enjoying and glorifying God, is to live a life surrendering my will to him. When you give up to God, you win. Now there is a paradox for you.

This paradox places one in a certain positive vantage point. From this vantage point it is hard not to be at least a little bit positive about life in general and one's life in particular, regardless of what's going on at any specific moment. So in a sentence you win the battle of life when you surrender to God. I think my friend's ability to place himself at a vantage point of eternal optimism that results in victorious living comes from his ability to "give up", every day of his life. That comes as somewhat of a surprise. Go figure. Or better yet, try it yourself. ⌒

STEALING EASTER

It's Easter weekend and the loons are back on Lac la Hache. It's fitting they should return at Easter. We share the lake with them spring, summer and fall. They are for us the sign of a new growing season, a new spring with all its good feelings and hope.

I never realized before, but the loon serves as our Easter lily, a kind of symbol for Easter that is a reminder in metaphorical terms of what the resurrection of Jesus Christ is all about. I heard the loon's haunting voice this morning as I lay in bed waiting for the house to warm up to the early morning fire. A long, lonely, labouring wail: an Easter symbol that speaks. The loon's presence: a metaphor for the new life and real hope the risen Christ promises. The loon's cry: a metaphor for God's creation that cries out in labour, waiting for the risen Christ to complete his redemptive work.

On Easter morning, we all left our beds early for an Easter egg hunt. As we were enjoying a breakfast of the fruit of our hunting, another hunt began on the lake not 50 meters from our house. Four juvenile eagles began to stalk our female loon.

This marauding troop of delinquents had been with us all last summer and had a habit of finding trouble, screaming defiantly as they soared over our house. Now they were in a circular flight pattern just a couple of meters over our loon, sweeping down to force the loon to dive and watching it swim for its life in the shallow clear water. As soon as the loon surfaced, the closest eagle swooped again. The loon frantically dived again. The eagles' strategy was obvious. Keep the loon under water until it drowned or tired to the point that one eagle could grab it. Soon an eagle dipped into the lake with its large yellow talons grabbing for the loon. The loon screamed and managed to squirm loose to begin the frantic process again. That was about all it could do. It could not get away because the lake had thawed for only a dozen meters around the shore. There was no room for an effective underwater escape into the deeper parts of the lake.

We could not take it any longer. Linda bolted out the door onto the deck, yelling and clapping her hands. I ran out the other door looking for rocks. The boys raced for the canoe and dumped it into the lake. The screaming eagles left reluctantly. Our loon headed for safer water with a new chance for life. Our Easter icon had made it through yet another attempt by the eagles to steal its life.

I reflected on the experience later that Easter while watching nine bald eagles standing on the ice in the centre of the lake. The incident reminded me that all around me there are predators waiting to steal Easter.

The first Christians personally experienced the risen Christ. John, Mary, Peter, Martha and Thomas all had personal encounters with

From Under a Blazing Aspen

the risen Christ on the first Easter. In those encounters, they were cared for personally. Doubt was dispelled, grief was defeated, unfaithfulness was forgiven, and love was given. Out of those personal relationships with the risen Christ, the first Christians experienced rebirth or newness in life.

Nearly 2,000 years later, Christians are still encountering the risen Christ in a spiritual and incarnational way, in a personal way. Out of our own relationship with the risen Christ, we receive care and rebirth to newness in life. This is our Easter experience.

All personal relationships take time and discipline. A relationship with the risen Christ is no different. The risen Christ is encountered in an especially personal way when you and I take our lives to Scripture, pause to talk with Christ in prayer, experience the care and love of Christ through time spent with another Christian. The risen Christ chooses to use these ways to maintain a personal relationship with you and me. They are such simple things, these means of grace, these carriers of Easter.

However, I am becoming increasingly aware of all kinds of predators that steal Easter from me by stealing my time with Christ. A career that can leave me totally fatigued is one example. Recreational activities that crowd in on every spare moment provide an example from the opposite end of the spectrum. Family that leave no space or time for me as an individual can be a third. A lack of discipline that seduces me into wasting time with a television – instead of "wasting time" with Christ – can be a fourth.

Make your own list of Easter stealers: Easter predators that scream at you and dominate your life. Then, as a project for spring, see what you can do about keeping these screaming eagles at bay. See what you can do to change the pattern. Don't let them keep you submerged and struggling for your life. ⌒

SLIP SLIDING AWAY

The trains didn't run yesterday. I wouldn't have noticed except Anne bought it to my attention. I had noticed the cause of the shutdown though. Tent caterpillars! As Linda, Chelsea and I were driving past the Quesnel area on our way up to Anne and Mike's ranch, we noticed that virtually every aspen tree was stripped of its usual lush spring foliage. The western forest tent caterpillar is only about an inch long but if you get enough of them together an entire forest can have its foliage eaten. And if you get enough of these seemingly innocuous little worms marching across a train track in their endless search for food, they can stop an entire train. It is a slippery and dangerous business trying to run a train up a grade greased with tent caterpillars. So they shut the trains down yesterday.

It is hard to believe that a glorified worm about two centimetres long and weighing less than a gram can stop a train several hundred metres long weighing mega-tonnes. Hard to believe, but true. On the way home from Mike and Anne's I got to thinking and this natural truth turned my mind to parable.

What is it about little things? They often seem to go unnoticed in my life. This seems particularly true with things that put the skids under my spiritual train. Let me give you an example.

Since giving my life to Christ about twenty years ago, it has been my desire to have a vibrant and consistent practice of contemplative prayer. It is my desire to have this as an integral part of my life because in my experience it is the greatest blessing one can have in this life. And so I have read all kinds of books on contemplative prayer, I have taken several courses in the spiritual disciplines, and I have, at times, greatly enjoyed periods when it is my daily practice to spend at least a half hour waiting on the Lord in contemplative and silent prayer.

And then along come the caterpillars. They put the skids under my daily discipline of blessing. They are usually tiny things like some esoteric bit of paperwork that I have convinced myself can't wait, or perhaps a late night that makes rising early difficult. These little distractions convince me to forgo my contemplative prayer time "for just one day". Before long one little thing has become two and then three; one day has become two and then a week and then a month. Finally, I realize my spiritual train has spun out completely.

I don't know about your discipleship but I have found in mine that it is not the big pitfalls that trap me. Rather, it's the little things that slip up on me unnoticed, often in concert with other little things. Before I know it I am slip-sliding away. I guess that is why Jesus warns us to "...keep watch and pray that you will not fall into temptation. The spirit is willing but the flesh is weak." (Mk.14:38) Jesus must have known about the tent caterpillars in my life.

From Under a Blazing Aspen

DRIVEN FROM THE LIGHT

It's April in the Cariboo, and aurora borealis season. The coming of the spring show of Northern Lights is something I look forward to with almost as much enthusiasm as the advent of fishing season. Ministry, at least the one that I am blessed with, quite often keeps me up at nights. One of the fringe benefits of my work-induced nocturnalism is an opportunity to imbibe in the unadulterated "blue northerns". Last night was a perfect example.

We exited the ranch house after worship, around 10:00 p.m. Linda packed Chelsea into the front of the pickup as I stuck the guitar and the box of church paraphernalia into the canopy and slammed the door. I worked at stuffing my girth behind the wheel of the truck and screwing myself down to the seat with the seatbelt. "Looks like another journey to the accompaniment of the Northern Lights rather than the radio. I don't mind them shining, but why do they have to render our radio impotent?" I grunted as I adjusted the seatbelt.

"You can get by without your usual four hours of Larry King on that stupid all-night American radio station. It barely comes in anyway. How you can listen to that drivel distorted by all the hissing and static I'll never know. I guess I won't be needing these tonight." Linda poked a pair of earplugs back into her purse and slouched in her seat as she spoke.

Both Chelsea and Linda were asleep about two hours later when I first noticed that things were not normal in the heavens. Rather than the yellows and blues of most Northern Lights displays, the sky was slashed with steaks of blood-red. At first, red shared the night sky with yellow and blue, dancing erotically with them. Then for no apparent reason red took over the whole sky. I was straining to look but I had a problem. The lights were in the northern sky and I was driving due south. I kept trying to look over my shoulder at what was turning out to be a rather unique performance of the "blue Northerns" changing their colour. However, no matter how much I worked at stealing a glance over my left shoulder or peering nearsightedly through the rearview mirror, I just could not get a satisfactory view. Eventually, Linda awoke for one of her backseat driver night checks and I drew her attention to what was taking place behind us in the heavens. She looked and gasped. She then began climbing around the cab of the pickup peering out every window that had a view to the north. "Wow! You really ought to stop the truck and get out so you can have a good look," she said.

We were still a good couple of hours from home. I was tired and looking forward to stuffing myself under a down comforter for a few hours of unconsciousness. Besides, I had a full day of work planned for tomorrow. That is why I just grunted and kept on driving, stealing frustrated glances over my shoulder. The Northern Lights continued to get more dazzling with each passing kilometer but I was too driven to stop and drink the sight in directly, too driven to face the amazing lights of the Easter sky.

A couple of hours more of driving and we finally droned to a halt before our home on the shores of Lac la Hache. It was 2:15 a.m. Linda lovingly lugged our sleeping little girl up the steps of the house. I debated with myself, down comforter or climb the hill? Finally, I hiked up to the top of the hill behind our place to a spot where I had a clear view of the night sky. The display of red Northern Lights had subsided considerably but they were still incredible. I stood there amazed.

Eventually, I made it to bed. I couldn't sleep. It was Easter and somehow my experience with the "red Northerns" unnerved me. Why had I been so driven that I would not stop the truck and face the Easter sky when it was at its most spectacular? What is it about being driven that causes one to miss the majesty of heaven's light? And what is it about being driven that renders one satisfied with furtive over-the-shoulder glances at the reflection of the glory of Easter's light, the Risen Christ? "Oh Risen One, grant me the grace to climb Easter's hill, face your glory directly and stand there AMAZED".

COMING FACE TO FACE WITH A MONSTER

When I was a kid, early spring meant sitting around Pete's potbellied stove and listening to my Dad and him swap lies about the bush. It was a delightful experience for an eight-year-old boy except for one thing. As the evening turned into night, the stories seemed to take a turn towards the scary. I found my attention stealing from the topic of discussion towards the single bare window of the shack. The window reflected the dim and only source of light, a coal oil lamp, in the most eerie way. I would try not to look at the window but my eyes were drawn to it like a magnet.

The more I stared at the bare window, the more I was convinced that a grizzly bear, the star of one of the previous tall tales, would suddenly loom up in the window and I would be face to face with a monster. I would shudder in fear, trying to resist the temptation to run. I would shake my head trying to dislodge the thought. I would turn my back on the window, trying to refocus my attention on the latest in the potbellied stove lying match. Nothing worked. Soon I was faking giant yawns in the hope that Dad would take pity on his poor tired son and take him home to the security of bright electric lights and curtains.

Coming face to face with a monster. It never really happened to me as a kid. It was just one of those fears that a kid with a souped-up imagination seems to be gifted with. But it happens to me now as an adult. Every so often, more often than I would like to admit, I come face to face with a monster. And the monster is me. What I mean is, I come face to face with myself as a sinner. It scares the hell out of me when it happens.

I try to use all the tricks I learned as a kid for dealing with monsters: things like running away from my sinful actions, shaking the realization of my sins out of my head, and turning my back on the reality of the sins I have committed to focus on something else. These remedies for monsters don't work any better now than they did when I was eight. Pretty soon I can't sleep, my life takes a turn towards the emptiness and fear that only guilt can bring and I realize that once again I have fallen into the slough of despond that John Bunyan wrote about in *Pilgrim's Progress*.

I came face to face with the monster again just the other day. Fortunate for me, I also came face to face with Al from out at Anahim Lake. We ran into one another in the hardware store in town. I don't know if my hair was standing on end from the last encounter with the monster, if sin's telltale look of guilt was written all over my face or if it was the Holy Spirit leading Al, but in the few minutes we spoke he shared something with me that proclaimed the gospel in a way that slew the monster. He shared how he was reading in the book of Romans recently where Paul says: "....where sin abounded, grace did much more abound."(Romans 5:20). Al said he had always read that passage as it applied to the fallen nature of all humanity. However, just the other day he'd realized that it applied to him personally. After our few words together, Al was off to Anahim Lake with his wife Julie and I was off to Lac la Hache with my thoughts.

As I thought about the passage from Romans that Al had shared with me, I also thought about another passage in the same book. Paul writes in the 7th chapter:

> "So I find it to be a law that when I want to do what is good, evil lies close at hand. For I delight in the law of God in my inmost self, but I see in my members another law at work with the law of my mind, making me captive to the law of sin that dwells in my members. Wretched man that I am! Who will rescue me from this body of death? Thanks be to God, through Jesus Christ our Lord" (Romans 7:21ff).

It seems Paul came face to face with the monster in himself as well. It also seems that Paul knew what Al found out and shared with me.

It is a disturbing Christian truth. It's not how much of a monster sin has made of me or you, the grace of God is always greater. The death Christ died on the cross was for my sin. Christ's death is sufficient for my forgiveness, no matter if my sins were of omission or commission, or if my sins were of word, thought or deed, or if my sin was large or small. Where sin abounds, grace much more abounds in God, through Jesus Christ. And, forgiven, I am called and empowered to put things right with those I sinned against.

Have you come face to face with any monsters lately, monsters that turned out to be sin in you? These words are faithful and true monster slayers:

> " If we say that we have no sin, we deceive ourselves, and the truth is not in us. If we confess our sin, he who is faithful and just will forgive us our sins and *cleanse us from all unrighteousness*" (1Jn.1:8ff).

ADVICE TO A NEOPHYTE

In the country, there is a lull between calving season and haying season. There is a lull between winter logging and summer logging. There is a lull between ice-fishing and spring fly-fishing. Having lived all my life in the country, I have come to look forward to this annual lull, better known as spring. It is a time when people with similar lifestyles and work concerns get together to talk and give advice. Being a country pastor is a bit of a problem. There tends not to be many of us around in the country, making it difficult to find someone of similar lifestyle and work concerns to swap advice with. This spring I remedied this by inventing my nephew Able. I decided to write him some advice as though it was coming from his uncle Willing.

Dear Able:

How time flies, dear nephew. It seems like it was only yesterday you were asking me for advice on how to get the little girl across the street to stop pulling your hair. Now you are graduating from Seminary and, it makes me proud, you are asking me for advice about ministry. I don't know if I am the best person to ask as I have never considered myself an exemplary minister. I simply enjoy what I do and what I do is simple. Ministry for me has always been the simple things in life. Things like loving, caring, sharing, praying and laughing. But you have asked me a specific question in your letter so I must focus on it: "What is the single most important thing I have learned about ministry?"

Let me try to answer your question by way of a little story. Not long after I had graduated from Seminary and was ordained, I met the most delightful elderly lady who taught me the most important thing that I needed to know about ministry. She was in the hospital and I was serving my rotation week as Hospital Chaplain. She asked to see a Chaplain and so it was that we met. She was very small and frail, with thin wispy white hair. She wore no upper teeth, which made her face extremely drawn and gaunt. The most remarkable things about her were her eyes. They sparkled and danced like moonlit waves on your favorite fishing lake back home. She never covered those eyes with glasses, which was quite remarkable for a person in her 87th year. You would have loved Mrs. Fraser.

We spent a lot of time together, Mrs. Fraser and I. I'm sure that I received far more from her than she ever did from me during our times together. I continued to come in to town to the hospital to visit with her long after my Chaplain week was over. Finally, she improved enough to go back home again. Regretfully, I sort of lost track of her.

It was one year later when we met again in exactly the same circumstance. I was Hospital Chaplain for the week and she was a patient needing a listener. This time, however, Mrs. Fraser was even more frail. Her white hair seemed to have thinned and become more wispy than ever. Her face was more sallow, thin and drawn than any I had ever seen. This time she was without both top and bottom teeth, giving her face an even more gaunt look than before. But those eyes of hers were the same un-spectacled dazzling dancing beauties that had the power to light up any heart that dared to look into them. I dared and was mesmerized. She talked and told story after delightful story. Then finally, one afternoon she got down to business.

"Will you do my funeral?" she blurted out. "I'm not to live much longer and I want to give my daughter a gift. The best thing I could give her right now is to plan my funeral." Dumbfounded and shocked, I nodded my head. Mrs. Fraser died the next day.

Three days later I was back in town at the undertaker's chapel "doing" Mrs. Fraser's funeral. I always thought myself to be rather good at funerals. The air of dignity at funerals appealed to my sense of importance and pur- pose. There was to be an open casket at the end of the service at the family's request. After the benediction, as is my custom in the case of an open casket, I came down from the pulpit with all the professional formality that I could muster and stood directly in front of the coffin, between it and the congregation, as the lid was opened. To my horror, the body in the coffin was not Mrs. Fraser's.

My heart surged into my throat as I looked at the cold waxy thing laying in the bed of satin and salal. This can't be happening, I thought as I stared at the darkhaired, bespectacled, rather plump-faced body before me. What should I do? My mind raced from calling out to the undertaker who had moved well back from the coffin by this time to the direct approach of diving forward and slamming the coffin shut before any of the family or friends could catch a glimpse of the bogus corpse. I finally settled on the chicken way out: stand aside, catch the people as they faint in the processional past the coffin and blame it all on the undertaker after it was over.

The family and friends filed past the coffin, kissing the body's cheek and patting its hand. I couldn't believe my eyes. I began to question if I was at the right funeral. My head was reeling and my eyes were fading to black when Mrs. Fraser's daughter came over and stood by me. "Oh Reverend, that was the most touching service…and Mom…you know, I haven't seen her look so good for ten years. She hardly ever wore her wig, glasses and teeth, you know." Somehow I remained standing.

After the interment service at the cemetery, I got behind the wheel of my car for the drive back to our home in the country. As I pulled out onto the road I had the distinct feeling that at least two people were having a good laugh in heaven. I know one of them was Mrs. Fraser and I suspect the other one was God. I couldn't help but join them. I laughed so hard I had to pull over to the side of the road. And there, as silence finally overtook me, I realized I had learned the most important thing in ministry. Never take yourself or what you do too seriously. After all, it is Christ who is at work in ministry. The Apostle Paul puts it best in 2 Cor. 4:7:

" We who have the spiritual treasure of the Gospel are like cracked pots, in order to show that the power of the Gospel belongs to God and not to us." (Please excuse the paraphrase).

I share this, dear nephew, as one "cracked pot" to another. I do hope that it will mean something to you in the years that lay ahead. It has meant much to me. At times, just knowing I can laugh at who I am and what I do has been the thread that has kept me reasonably sane and continuing in ministry.

With the Master's love

Your Uncle, Willing.

GRANDPA CHARLIE'S CHALLENGE

One early spring day about five years ago, I had the occasion, while doing some deputation work among the churches of Vancouver Island, to go out to the west coast. I visited one of the beaches near Tofino. The sea was crashing on the beach and just offshore, about three kilometers out, small boats were struggling to make their way through some pretty rough water. I lay down with my back propped against a large piece of driftwood to enjoy the deserted beach and the powerful sea. Soon I was daydreaming. And in my daydreams, my thoughts were pulled towards my mentor, at least in spirit, Great-Grandpa Charlie. Grandpa Charlie had sailed these very waters a long time ago. It was fitting to feel close to him as I sat and stared at the sea.

I never knew Great-Grandpa Charlie, but I wished I had. You see, Great-Grandpa Charlie was an ordained Methodist circuit preacher at the turn of the century. For much of his early ministry he wandered up and down the rugged coastline of BC taking the church of Christ to the isolated logging, mining and fishing camps and bands of native people that then dotted our coastline. The only method of travel was the treacherous Pacific Ocean, so it became his highway.

The mission ship, the *Udahl*, became his home. The native people he visited called him "The Rev. Charlie On The Sunday Come To Jesus Boat". More than once the Rev. Charlie nearly went to Jesus prematurely, for the waters of the Pacific coast were treacherous and the *Udahl* wasn't much more than a glorified rowboat. In 1908 the *Udahl* sank in Queen Charlotte Sound. Great-Grandpa Charlie escaped with only his mouth organ. Everything else went down with the ship. Charlie and Captain William Oliver lived on an island for three months, guests of some benevolent native people. Once they were found by search parties from home, they went right to work procuring another mission boat, the *Homespun*. Before the year's end, Charlie and Captain William Oliver were back on the treacherous sea again.

I have Great-Grandpa Charlie's diary from the last year he spent on the coastal mission. On Thursday, April 14th, 1910, there is an entry that is fairly typical:

"Left Port Simpson for Portland Canal ...ran for about 4 hours ...storm met us so we had to run for shelter ...ran about 10 miles into William's Bay ...storm blew water off the high waves like dust ...weighed anchor 1:30 PM for Hamilton's Cannery in Dogfish Bay ...intended anchoring there but at 9 PM had to get out from there ...too rough ...ran to Tombstone Bay through blinding snowstorm ...anchored about 1:00 AM."

Great-Grandfather's diary is full of descriptions of days like this. As I have read, I find myself often wondering what would make a middle-aged man who lived very comfortably in the society of Victorian

England uproot his family and move to the wilderness of Cape Scott, BC. What would motivate a man to bounce up and down the treacherous coast of BC all year long, visiting native villages, logging camps, fish-canneries and mining towns to sing and say a few things about Jesus? What made him do it? Was it a sense of adventure or a big stipend or was he just a fool?

I take some personal comfort that my Methodist Great-Grandfather was not alone. Christ's church had, in all of its denominational expressions, multitudes of men and women doing similar kinds of mission work at that time and at just as much personal risk and cost. My own Presbyterian denomination, led by the missionary zeal of James Robertson, our Missions Superintendent at the turn of the century, had numerous missionaries going out to people whom they perceived needed Christ. In those days, wherever there were people living on the Canadian frontier there was the missionary, bringing Christ and His church, in one form or another, into rural homes, barns half built, community halls and camp tents.

A story is told about James Robertson by his biographer Charles Gordon in his book, *The Life of James Robertson.*

It seems that Robertson rode into a prairie town one Saturday night. Being determined to hold a worship service on the following morning, Robertson asked if the local hotel owner would be kind enough to procure a suitable place for worship. The hotel owner said he would oblige. The following morning, Robertson showed up at the bar where men were still enthusiastically imbibing. He asked the hotel owner, who was tending the bar, if he had found a suitable place for the planned Sunday worship. The bartender replied with a wink at his inebriated patrons, " Sure thing, pard. Here is your congregation. Step right up behind the bar and let fly. God knows they need it."

Robertson did just that, without hesitation and to some effect. He was first treated to a chorus of jeers, then a chorus of singing as he led them in a hymn, and then after his sermon, a chorus of pleas for a missionary to be sent out fulltime. One was sent forthwith.

What motivated James Robertson to leave the safety and comforts of urban Ontario to preach sermons in smoky smelly bars and God knows where else across Canada's frontier at the turn of the century? What made him willing to practice such an uncomfortable brand of ministry? Was it a sense of adventure? Was James Robertson a fool?

There is a point to all of this historical nostalgia. Most of us have been taught that what the church did at the turn of the century was driven by faulty theology that equated the church with the Kingdom of God. We have been taught that what the church did at the turn of the century was imperialistic and sociologically detrimental, particularly to native peoples. We have been taught to discount the church of this age of missionary zeal. Perhaps we should. But I for one still find myself haunted by Great-Grandpa Charlie and his motivation.

From reading and pondering Great-Grandpa's diary, I suspect that what motivated him, and others like him, to give up the comforts of home for the risks of the treacherous sea or a pulpit in a seedy smelly bar and a bed in someone's hayloft was the conviction that the gospel of Christ was the most important thing in the world. They believed that faith in Christ had the power to bring healing, wholeness,

From Under a Blazing Aspen

salvation and justice to bear on one's life. They believed that they had a mission in life, a mission to share Christ with the world, at any cost. Sometimes they erred in carrying out their mission. That is the cost of being human. But they were right on when it came to motivation and focus: Christ for the world.

Do you know what? I'm afraid. I'm afraid that we North American Christians don't believe this Jesus stuff anymore -- that somehow we have lost our Christocentric motivation and our focus on the world. We seem to have become a people motivated by fear of institutional failure and have adopted tinkering with church structure as our focus and mission. My own denomination is a good example. In the past three decades, Lamp Reports have been followed with Committees To Double In The Eighties which have been followed by Church Growth Committees which have been followed by Restructuring Committees which have been followed by State Of The Church Committees which have been followed with Think Tanks. We have just spent over a million "mission dollars" on restructuring the national church offices, only to discover that the restructured church does not suit us. Now, according to a recent Think Tank report, we need to do it again, this time more much more radically. This time of course we will do it right.

I am not going to criticize these processes or its participants, although it is very tempting. I have too much respect for the many people I know who were involved in these processes in various denominations. However, I have one thing I feel compelled to say. I want to say it on behalf of Great-Grandpa Charlie and our mission-minded forefathers and mothers now silenced by the passage of time. I am saying it as a present-day missionary who desperately needs the support of the whole church in order to maintain my motivation and focus. What I say is this.

I challenge each of us to resist the temptation of trying to save our beloved institution by fiddling with its structure or polity. I challenge each of us to stop wasting our resources and focus all our time and energy on bearing Christ, in word and action, to the world.

Grandpa Charlie might have said it like this, "Enough already. Get on with being People Of God." Sociologists like Reginald Bibby tell us that people everywhere are parched for spiritual direction and truth. They should be our focus, not ourselves. We are called to be the bearers of living water, not thirsters for institutional success.

A POSTSCRIPT FROM THE SECULAR WORLD

After going through several restructuring processes in government institutions, post-secondary educational institutions and business institutions, I have learned the hard lesson that if the mission focus of any institution is right and if the people within the institutional structure are committed to that focus and motivated by it, they will make any institutional structure work well. If focus and motivation are missing, it does not matter how neat and new the management flowchart looks, the institution will be ineffectual. It is not institutional structure or polity but the focus and motivation of the people within the institution that are the keys to accomplishing a mission.

Summer

BROTHER TO A GRASSHOPPER

Last summer we returned to Ta Ta Creek. I know. "Where in the world is Ta Ta Creek?" It's home, that's where -- the source of our roots. Linda and I spent the first 18 to 20 years of our lives roaming the hills of Ta Ta Creek.

While we were back, I took a couple of long walks to some of my favourite old haunts: down by the culvert where I fished for bass, along the old road by the swamp where I spent most of my time as a boy, up the old toboggan hill that still scares me when I stand on its summit.

A spray of grasshoppers shooting out from my path accompanied me everywhere I went, just as they did when I was ten. Ta Ta Creek becomes Grasshopper Corners on a dry summer's day. When I was a kid, they served as objects of my science experiments, the first candidates for my bug collection and, most importantly, a ready supply of bass bait. From a grasshopper's perspective, a ten-year-old boy on the hunt is an insurmountable problem. Helpless creatures, those grasshoppers. Sometimes I feel we are brothers.

Let me try to explain. Often I feel like Moses and the Israelites must have felt when they left Egypt and made their tear-streaked trek across the desert. They found themselves camped on the edge of the land God promised to give them. Moses sent out one group of spies to look at what lay ahead. Two contradictory reports came back.

Most of the spies reported:

> "The land through which we have gone, to spy it out, is a land that devours its inhabitants; and all the people we saw in it are of great stature...we seemed to ourselves like grasshoppers, and so we [must] have seemed to them" (Num. 13:32 RSV).

The future seemed an impossible challenge, full of insurmountable problems. They felt as vulnerable as grasshoppers hunted by a ten-year-old scientist, bug collector and bass fisherman. That's how I feel many times as I ponder what lies ahead of me in my life and ministry. Being brother to a grasshopper is part of my Christian experience. To be honest, I'm not too fond of it.

A second minority report by Joshua and Caleb stated the opposite of the majority:

> "The land we passed through, to spy it out, is an exceedingly good land. If the Lord delights in us, he will bring us into this land and give it to us...Do not fear the [huge] people...the Lord is with us" (Num. 14:7-10 RSV).

Amazingly, both reports came from looking at the same land. The difference was not in what was seen but in how it was seen. The "brother to a grasshopper" group saw what lay ahead without God. Joshua and Caleb saw what lay ahead with God. Joshua and Caleb saw a future where, despite problems, God would be leading and fully present. This encouraged them to advise the Israelites to risk going ahead. The Israelite people listened to the grasshopper brothers. They turned back out of fear to 40 more years of desert wandering.

Every morning I wake up and ponder some aspect of the future. It may be the next day, week, month or year. The future can make me feel like a brother to a grasshopper. Insurmountable problems can make me desire to stay where I am or even turn back out of fear. It can, if I look at a future where God is absent and provides no leadership. I can, however, perceive the future as Joshua and Caleb did. I can accept Christ at his word, "Lo, I am with you always, to the close of the age" (Matthew 28:20). From now on, when I begin to grow antennae and long legs, I'll check where I have put God. Likely I'll have left him in my past, out of my present and future. To defeat grasshopperitis quickly, remember:

"The Lord is with us [always]" (Num. 14:9 RSV).

IT HAPPENS IN THE STRANGEST PLACES

We had been driving for what seemed like days. The boys, weary of bouncing in the back seat of the crew cab pickup, changed over to riding their mountain bikes. They were able to go as fast as we could over the four-wheel drive trail that served as our road to our destination, Chaunigan Lake. We still had another couple of hours of low range 4 x 4 bouncing when a couple of hundred metres below our road a lake appeared. This was not just any lake, but a beautiful jewel of water clasped by the towering Chilcotin mountains. The setting was enhanced by a small wilderness campsite tucked into a peaceful bay. It was not where we were going but it was where we ended up. Darkness helped us decide to make camp.

Morning found us in the teeth of an icy gale lashing out from the gigantic Homathko Icefield a few kilometers to the west. The frigid wind sent us searching for sweaters and longing for long-johns. Tsuniah Lake, our non-destination, was producing waves you could surf on. Launching our canoe and fishing was out of the question. Lighting a campfire and lounging around it with a good book was beyond the realm of reason. It was hard to find any rationale for staying a minute longer at Tsuniah Lake. Typically, we held a family conference, took a vote and stayed a week.

It was a strange setting for a week of summer vacation. It was a strange place for mission and ministry. That it did, and wonderfully I might add, I can only credit to the workings of an ever-present Christ who is not limited by any human classification of "strange".

There were two other groups sharing the wind, waves and campsite with us. One man had a seaworthy metal boat which he offered to take me out in so I could fish. We spent several hours bouncing off large waves and talking. He had not had anything to do with Christ or His church and to find himself confined to a fishing boat with a minister of Christ's church was strange for him. He was surprised to find how down-to-earth Christ and one of his ministers could be. We shared many significant hours and I really enjoyed his friendship. For him, I'm sure it was the beginning of the opening of the door of faith.

The other party of campers included a man who was a graduate of a Christian seminary and who was in his last year of finishing a Ph.D he had been working on intermittently for years. He was tired and frustrated with his studies. We spent quite a bit of time talking about Christ, ministry and fishing. I know it stimulated and encouraged me and I'm quite sure it did him too. I think we both left Tsuniah Lake with healing and new energy for life and work, not to mention coolers packed with tasty rainbow trout.

Late in the summer, as I reflect on this week of summer vacation that became mission and ministry, I find myself reminded of what I have

come to believe is the essence of Christian mission. It is by defini-
tion the ministry of Christ and His church directed to the outsider. It
is ministry or service done, not for the Church's benefit, but for the
world's. You and I don't choose the exact location, the time or the
people for Christian ministry with the world. If we did, nine times
out of ten we would choose to do it only within the church. Mission
would amount to getting people into the church, where we could be
comfortable in caring for them and making demands of stewardship.
Most church growth endeavours err towards this self-serving attitude. With mission, attitude is crucial. Christ is concerned first with
the world, with the outsider. The church is His chosen vehicle to
reach out to the world in selfless, Christ-like ways, for the world's
benefit. That is the church's mission.

That Christ chooses what seems to be strange times, places and people for mission and ministry, usually outside the Church, does not
surprise me as much as it once did. After all it was this same Christ
who chose to practice his ministry in some rather strange places with
some rather different people, outsiders all. In fact, I am coming to
expect Christ to surprise me when it comes to mission, its place,
purpose and people. ⌒

EDGES

I mind the time I climbed the Nurse's Face. Actually, I really do mind the time I climbed the Nurse's Face. Linda and I grew up five miles from one another under the shadow of the Nurse's Face. This Rocky Mountain peak is just under 9000 ft above sea level, and it towers above the main valley of the Rocky Mountain Trench by about 6500 feet. It is one of the taller and more spectacular mountains in the local area. In the summer all of the snow leaves the face of the peak except for a spot to mark an eye and a slash to mark a nurse's hat, hence its name.

From the time I was five I wanted to climb this mountain. It wasn't until I was 21 that I got to do it. It took me that long to find a climbing partner, my wife of one year. Linda was a couple of years younger than I, still in her teens, and I considered her to be my junior in years and in all things, including mountain climbing. So as we set off from the end of the mining road to climb the face, I was in the lead with the rope and the jaunty air of a leader of a major alpine expedition. I was doing rather well with my jaunty air on the scree slopes below. I wasn't doing all that badly on the rough climbing over small outcrops on the mid-slopes.

It was on the last third of the slope that my jaunty air kind of evaporated, along with just about every desire I ever had to climb "that stupid mountain", or any mountain for that matter. We were roped together and making our way up a cliff where every second handhold seemed to crumble under the slightest pressure and crash on the rocks below. I was terrified. As expedition leader I informed my junior partner and wife that we must not go any further as it was too dangerous. My junior partner informed me that it was not too dangerous, I was just a chicken. Besides, she said that she was not going back down when she had already come two-thirds of the way up. I told her this was faulty female logic. She scowled with some disgust, climbed the cliff past me and continued on up the face of the mountain.

What could I do? I was too terrified to go down by myself. The rope that was my only security was disappearing up the cliff with my darling young wife attached to it. I did the only thing I could do. With whimpers of "wait for me, hon" coming from between clenched teeth and with my last vestige of courage, not to mention pride, I scrambled the remaining third of the way up the Nurse's Face behind my junior partner.

Three things happened as we sat on the edge of the cliff at the top of the mountain that day. Linda lost every vestige of *junior* in the partnership which is our marriage. I lost my lunch to the accompaniment of Linda's enthusiastic babbling about familiar features of the local landscape seen previously only from ground level. And I learned something about me and edges.

From Under a Blazing Aspen

Edges make me feel extremely uncomfortable! It does not matter if it is the edge of a mountain cliff or the edge of experience where the unknown begins, or the edge of life where death begins, I am not partial to edges. There is a definite edge to the Gospel. For me at least, this means there is a definite discomfort to it.

In the Old Testament you can get a feel for what I am talking about in the call stories of the Prophets. A good example is the call story of Jeremiah found in the first ten verses of the book that bears his name. Jeremiah is called by God to proclaim Old Testament gospel. He is able to see the edge to his calling as well as the edge to what he must proclaim. He is told by God that God has chosen him, set him apart to proclaim, and appointed him as an agent of gospel since before he was conceived. There is an uncomfortable edge if I have ever encountered one. It is the edge to the will of God for a person. The edge that refuses "no" as an answer, will not be denied, will give one a choice but only one thing to choose.

Jeremiah tries to say, "No, I am too young... I don't have anything to say... I don't know how to say it."

God says, " 'No' is not an acceptable answer. Besides, I am with you to deliver you."

You can almost hear Jeremiah say, "Deliver me? Deliver me? You mean on top of all the uncomfortable edges around the sovereign will of God, people are going to be after my neck?"

God says, "That pretty much sums it up. You see, Jeremiah, you are going to speak for me. And you will speak harshly about justice and faithfulness before you will speak tenderly about comfort and new life." Oh, the edge to God's Gospel and the claims it puts on one's life!

Six hundred years later, Jesus walks out of the desert into his hometown of Nazareth. The story is told by all Synoptic Gospel writers. Upon invitation, Jesus stands up in church one Saturday and reads from the scroll of Isaiah a passage of Scripture that everyone knows anticipates the coming of Messiah. As was the custom, Jesus then sat to preach the sermon. His proclamation made it clear that in Jesus the messianic prophesies were fulfilled once and for all.

This hometown boy, son of a local carpenter, one whom everyone knew in town, one whom everyone watched grow up through noisy messy diapers to beardless adulthood, he is Messiah? The people try to throw him off a cliff.

Oh, the edge to the gospel of God when it is held up right in front of your face but does not live up to your expectations. Oh, the uncomfortable edge to the gospel when it must be proclaimed in action and word at the personal risk of rejection and dismissal at the hands of friends, relatives and neighbours that you have known most of your life. Oh, the discomfort of the content of the gospel that shows God on the side of the outsider, the powerless and the oppressed, and demands that we stand there with Him.

POSTSCRIPT

I dislike the discomfort of edges as much today as I did 28 years ago on that mountaintop. However, the time that has painted grey into my beard has also given me the ability to perceive colour where before there was only form. Edges have become less about discomfort and more about the fullness and nuances of life. I have noticed that the gospel always seems to bring me to the edge where it is uncomfortable but where life is very real and often very rich. ⌒

ISAIAH'S EAGLE CAN SWIM

"What on earth is that silly eagle doing now?" Linda's surprised tone of voice brought me running out of the bedroom still hitching up my pants. The pair of bald eagles who nested on the island immediately opposite our Cariboo lakefront home were always up to something interesting. Most often it was something different; it was usually something predatory and opportunistic. I had started referring to them as "white-headed buzzards" about a month after we began to share the lakeshore with them.

"What's he doing this time?" I asked as I blindly hunted for my glasses.

"I haven't a clue," said Linda. "He was in the top of that big spruce tree right beside our dock and all of a sudden he just fell in the water like he had a heart attack or something. Look there, he's just sitting in the water as stunned as a drunken duck."

I somehow managed to get finished with my pants, found my glasses and perched them on my nose. The majestic bird was still sitting half-submerged with only its neck and head above the water. It was about ten feet from our dock looking dazed and shaken. I was about to find a canoe paddle to go down and effect a rescue, or at least a mercy killing, when Linda began to laugh.

"Will you look at that," she said. "The silly thing is doing the backstroke. And look at the loons. They are moving in for the kill."

Sure enough, that was exactly what was happening. The eagle was using its wings to swim powerfully backwards towards the island on the far side of the lake. The loons were howling their heads off, circling the eagle and at times diving right underneath it. Two more loons from the bay just up from us also came to torment the waterbound eagle. It looked like the Canadian loon was about to finally get the better of the American eagle. A wicked little grin was beginning to form at the corner of my mouth. God knows how many baby loons the old eagle had killed since we had been living on the lakeshore.

By this time the eagle was just hitting his stride. He was powerfully rowing with his wings like an Olympic sculler, at times looking over his shoulder to keep his line straight. He didn't seem to be the slightest bit concerned about the loons; there was the mark of purpose in his actions and not the slightest hint of panic. Somewhat disappointed, I said to Linda, "That crafty old buzzard has this all planned. He is up to something. We'll just have to watch what happens when he reaches the island."

Sure enough, after about ten minutes of steady rowing, the eagle hit the shore of the island. Without pausing he hopped out of the water pulling a huge sucker fish up onto the beach with his talons. Through the binoculars we watched as he commenced breakfast. When he

From Under a Blazing Aspen

had eaten enough to satisfy himself and lighten the load, he grasped what was left of the fish in his talons and flew heavily up to the nest where young eaglets were waiting for their Cariboo version of "breakfast at the CN Tower".

As I was driving to a house church gathering later in the day, I found myself reflecting upon our eagle experience and upon Scripture. One of my touchstones is Isaiah 40:31:

> "...they who wait upon the Lord shall renew their strength, they shall mount up with wings as eagles..."(KJV).

I had always thought of this metaphor in terms of an eagle soaring in the sky. The promise of human strength coming from God being like the powerful eagle soaring in his element is rich. But now it was somehow richer. What about the strength of an eagle swimming powerfully across a lake with its wings, completely out of its element, radically out of the zone of its usual comfort and safety? The promise of strength from God being like that is profound, for it is strength that is adaptable, strength that is effectual in places of risk.

So often I have evaluated the presence of the strength of God in terms of how safe and comfortable I feel. This scant sense of the strength of God has often limited me to my own zones of comfort and the kind of life where I do not have to take any risks. But, if Isaiah's eagle can swim, and I now know it can, the strength promised from God is adaptable, effectual in any situation, supportive of risktaking and present even when I have taken a plunge into the unknown. It almost moves me to take up skydiving in my old age. Well, wait just a minute!

INVISIBLE CURRENTS

I sat looking out the window trying to understand. Less than an hour ago when I gazed out at the bay the water was as smooth as glass. A loon swimming by made the only surface ripple on the little bay which feeds Eagle Creek into Canim Lake. But when a slight breeze puffed across the lake, suddenly the silky-smooth surface of the bay changed dramatically. As I watched, it was broken with a swell that had waves two feet high running through the centre of the bay only, in a strip from the mouth of Eagle Creek out into the lake for about 200 meters. Other than the strip of waves, there was virtually no other wave action. The rest of the bay and lake was pebbled with tiny wavelets that glinted in the afternoon sun like diamonds. I opened the lodge window to see if there was some freakish wind blowing in strips. There was only the gentlest of breezes coming across the lake and caressing the tall spruce trees at its edge.

So what on earth was the power source behind the two-foot waves in the center strip of the bay? I sat looking and figuring but nothing made any sense. The only thing that had changed in the past half hour was the advent of the ever-so-gentle breeze that produced the tiny twinkling wavelets on the rest of the lake. Finally I went down the stairs of the lodge to the eating area. I asked Joyce as she served my supper, "What's the secret to the isolated strips of two-foot waves in the middle of the bay?" I tried to hide my puzzled intrigue behind an aura of nonchalance.

Joyce said, "Oh that...it always happens with the wind, the slightest breeze blowing against the usually invisible current of Eagle Creek as it enters the bay."

The usually invisible current of Eagle Creek? This was the source of the power that created waves two feet high in an otherwise relatively calm bay? When there was no wind, the current was invisible as the creek flowed out into the bay. However, with even the slightest breeze blowing against the current you had two-foot waves that spoke volumes about the power of the current of Eagle Creek.

Later I tested Joyce's theory. When the bay was perfectly smooth again and there was no wind at all, I went down to the lake. I made sure no one was looking and casually cast a stick into where I had seen the waves the afternoon before, the afternoon of the breeze. Sure enough, the stick took off out into the smooth lake like a goosed trout. The powerful current of Eagle Creek was there all the time. It was just invisible unless a wind blew against it. I was moved to think in parables -- about the power of God always streaming into my life, and about the winds of affliction. (2Cor.12:7-10).

MAYBE YOU LEARN SOMETHING TOO!

Seeking An Earthy Christian Spirituality

Setting One: a beautiful church sanctuary two blocks south of the West Edmonton Mall. About seventy of us from various Christian churches had gathered for a week of study on native spirituality. I had come to this workshop hoping to gain some much-needed insight into traditional native spirituality and its appreciation for the earth. I knew that native spirituality took creation seriously. I wanted to learn how, as a rural person, I could begin to develop my Christian spirituality in a way that respected the earth rather than insisted on dominion over it. What better way to get a leg up on thinking about this stuff than a week-long workshop with other Christians seeking similar theological knowledge?

About one day into the workshop I could tell something was wrong. There was only one native person involved and she was a well-educated Christian nun from back east. Everyone else was as white as the driven snow. Most were, as far as I could tell, from urban churches. Pretty soon an urban agenda began to take charge. One resource person spent a lot of our time trying to turn native spirituality into feminist theology. Another whole afternoon was spent trying to turn native spirituality into postmodern Christianity. Yet another afternoon was spent developing a cosmic Jesus because a white male Jewish Jesus didn't fit in well with the guilt that one of the resource people felt concerning what white 19th-century Christian evangelists did to Indians.

"Shiiiiit," I said to my wife at our campsite on the edge of town. "Let's go to the West Edmonton Mall. I'm sure I will learn more about native spirituality there than in this workshop." So we left the cosmic postmodern feminist Jesus folks and went swimming in the West Edmonton Mall. As I watched our two boys try to commit suicide on a half-dozen different water slides, I tried to figure out why on earth the workshop hadn't been held at any one of a dozen rural Indian reserves that existed within 30 minutes of Edmonton, using native elders as resource people.

My West Edmonton Mall version of continuing education took place eight years ago. It was the last time I took a continuing education course from the Christian church. Every year I await the continuing education offerings of the various theological schools and other organizations with great anticipation. Every year I open the advertisements that come across my desk with much excitement. Every year I throw the advertised offerings in the garbage with disgust. As I go through this annual ritual, I am developing an increasing awareness of how urbanized the Christian church is and how this directly affects my ability as a rural person to develop as a Christian.

I am a rural person. I was born that way. I live that way. I speak that way. My ministry is that way. With any providence at all, I will die that way. My way at looking at things, my interests, my needs and my life all reflect this country existence. And, like it or not, it is distinctly different from the urban or suburban experience. The resources of an increasingly urbanized Christian church are not serving rural Christians like me at all well.

Setting Two: a rural remote Shuswap Indian reserve one year later. I walked up the hill from the archaeological site where government archaeologists were supervising excavation work on a prehistoric native pit house. In the distance I caught the sound of someone chanting and drumming. Instinctively I moved toward the heart beat of the drum sounds. As I came over the rise of a hill above the creek I finally caught sight of him. He was older, dressed in jeans and a beat-up black felt cowboy hat with an eagle feather dangling down his back. His cowboy boots were red and badly worn. He was beating an empty two-litre plastic Coke bottle against his knee to produce the drum noise. Silently I walked up to his cooking fire in front of his tent. Two young women were cooking bannock on the open fire. The bannock was golden brown and smelled good.

The old Indian smiled at me with a toothless grin, stopped drumming and nodded. "Nice bannock," I said after a long silence. He said something in Salish and pointed at the bannock. I tried to repeat it but my tongue got in the way. He said it again. I tried again and he laughed. I walked over to him and sat on the grass next to his plastic lawn chair in front of his old Sears umbrella tent. He said the word again, slower this time. When I tried again, I must have come pretty close to saying it right as he nodded kindly to me. It was the last word I spoke for over an hour.

"Anyone can sing and dance Indian music," he said. "It is music that comes from the heart. For nine months you are next to your mother's heart. Boom boom, boom boom. The beat is as natural as life. It is music of the heart that you learn from your mother. It is the same with us and this land. The earth is our mother. She teach us from her heart. You see those trees over there? They are as the hair on your head. They are part of me. And that grass on that knoll. It is as your skin. It is part of me. The earth is our mother. We are people of the land. We are related to it and all the rocks, earth, water and living things that make up the land. It is like this circle. To the south of the circle are the finned ones. To the east are the feathered ones. To the west are the four-legged ones. To the north are the insect ones. Each one is cared for by our earth mother. They are like relations to us. Our earth mother feed us. She raise us. She love us. She cause us to sing. She teach us. She teach us to be humble and love the land and the animals. If we hurt the land we hurt our mother. Our mother will always have the last word."

The old Indian elder went on talking and I sat there on the grassy hill drinking in the solitude, the aroma of his aspen cooking fire and the deep spiritual teachings he gave about the land and the people of the land. Finally he said, "I bet you wished you brung a pencil, huh?"

I nodded and looked quietly from him to the land behind him. He had so much to teach me about spirituality and the land. Me, with a Masters of Divinity degree and one in forestry. Me, an ordained minister in the Christian church. Me, a lifelong rural person. In his presence I sensed how little I really knew about the land and the spirit.

From Under a Blazing Aspen

"Maybe some time you come my place. Maybe you and me go on to the mountain four-five days. Maybe you and me, we talk on that mountain. Maybe the earth mother teach you too. Maybe you learn something that help you live in your world too. Maybe you learn something too."

Spirituality and land. It has become increasingly clear to me that the Christian spirituality since the Industrial Revolution has lost its connection with the earth. The Industrial Revolution resulted in a separation of people from the land, burying them in cites to be used as a workforce. Not only that, the earth, once the nurturing centre for farming peoples, became primarily a raw material for factories with little spiritual value and maximum perceived economic potential.

The Christian church became a willing captive of the Industrial Revolution a long time ago. It was urbanized and industrialized to the point that its practice, spirituality and theology was forever changed. In fact the Christian church of the last few centuries worked hard to provide a suitable theological foundation for the formation of cities, factories and the subjugation of land and people. The theology exported to the Americas was this urbanized and industrialized version. No wonder it clashed with the land and the people of the land who lived there. And it is still clashing.

As a rural Christian, I have to be aware that my spirituality and theology is incomplete. I must also become aware that I will find little help in fleshing it out from the urbanized and industrialized Christian church, for it is just as much captive now as ever. I will have to take the risk of finding help for my spiritual quest from the land and its native people. I must risk being taught by the elders of the people of the land, my native friends. ⌒

LIKE A RING OF BRIGHT WATER

"That's queer!"

"What on earth are you talking about?" said Linda.

"There's an unidentified flying object floating on the lake," I said.

"You mean a spaceship on pontoons? Sometimes I really wonder about your imagination." Linda left her morning coffee and got up from the kitchen table to join me at the window.

We pushed our noses closer to the window and peered out into the summer morning sunlight. Sure enough, what we saw was a ring with sparkling lights glinting through windows all around its edges. It looked like a flying saucer floating on the water. "See, I told ya," I quipped with glee.

Linda stared through a frown at the ring with its glistening lights floating down Lac la Hache. "That's not a flying saucer," she said. "It's some kind of animal. In fact it's more than one."

"It doesn't look like any animal I've ever seen. If it ain't a flying saucer its gotta be some kind of huge diamond ring. It's perfectly round and the sun is glinting off diamonds set all around the ring." My imagination was about to speed shift into overdrive. However before I could give it maximum throttle and start hypothesizing about the slighted giant that threw the ring in the lake after being rejected by the maiden of Lac la Hache, Linda ruined everything and went after the binoculars.

"It's a ring of otters," Linda exclaimed. "Awww, look at them. It's just like in Gavin Maxwell's book *Ring Of Bright Water.*"

When we looked through the binoculars we could see a family of otters with all the adults, about five of them, lying on their backs in a perfect circle. Every so often an adult would dive down in the centre of the ring and come up with a small fish or a freshwater mussel. After the successful hunt, it would find its place back in the circle and put the food on its stomach to clean and prepare it for eating.

Meanwhile in the centre of the circle there were several young otters, about four we estimated. They were totally engrossed in playing, diving and splashing. It was the droplets of water from their playing that was catching the morning sunlight, glinting like diamonds. Every so often, one of the young otters would approach one of the adults in the outer circle and would receive a piece of food.

From the deck, where we had moved for a better view, we could hear that this ring of bright water was anything but silent. A background of chuckling , blowing and cooing seemed to give the whole thing an aura of song and contentment. We also noticed that the ring exuded a sense of providence and security. Not only was the ring a centre for food procurement and sharing but there was something about it that seemed to say to the eagles roosting on the dead snag on the island opposite our house that this group of animals was not to be messed with. Normally, the ever-predatory eagles would swoop from their roost to investigate whatever looked vulnerable, either on the lake or on the shoreline. One time, we even saw them check out our old dog while she was playing on the lawn by the lake. But although the eagles were perched at battle stations this morning, they didn't show the slightest interest in the ring of bright water.

Much of the rest of the morning was consumed by watching the ring of bright water as it was moved slowly down the lake by a gentle breeze. It was so fascinating that when it eventually drifted from our view, Linda and I were tempted to get into the Chestnut canoe and sneak along the shore to continue our observations. That we did not succumb to temptation was due to a house church meeting that was expecting us at Nazko, three hours drive to the north.

The afternoon drive, much of it in the silence of friendship, was time for processing the natural history observations of the morning. As so often happens to me when I contemplate nature, eventually my thoughts took the morning's observations for a wander through Scripture.

Scripture is full of words and metaphors that seek to describe the church or a people of God. There is the Apostle Paul's "body of Christ" metaphor in the Christian writings of Scripture -- or is it an allegory? There are the word pictures in the Hebrew Scriptures for "my people" and "house of Israel". The list is extensive in both

Testaments, each word picture or metaphor conveying something rich in terms of people's relationships to each other and to their God. After spending the morning watching the otters and the afternoon taking the otter experience into Scripture, I could not help thinking in parable about the church.

What is the church like? What metaphor should we use to help us appreciate it? The church is like a ring of bright water, a family of otters. The ring is formed by the mature and wise. By experience they know what is dangerous and how to provide care. They form the ring for protection, nurture and to define a space for the younger and less experienced to be free to play and learn. Those of the outer circle provide nurture and teaching. Those inside the circle, the young ones, provide freedom of thought and action that brings joy and beauty to all, just as the sun turns the splashing of the otters' exuberant energy into the likes of diamonds. The otters' ring is formed in the water. Water is the medium by which each otter finds its way into the ring. Although the water is not the ring, it is crucial for its formation. So what is the church like? It is like a ring of bright water.

From Under a Blazing Aspen